The Home Farming Revolution
for Drylands

By Zoe Wilcox and Melanie Rubin

Copyedited by Kay Bird with Melanie Rubin and SpeedReadAmerica

Front and back cover photography: kylezimmermanphotography.com
Cover design: Kyle Zimmerman and Liliana Gonzalez Garcia

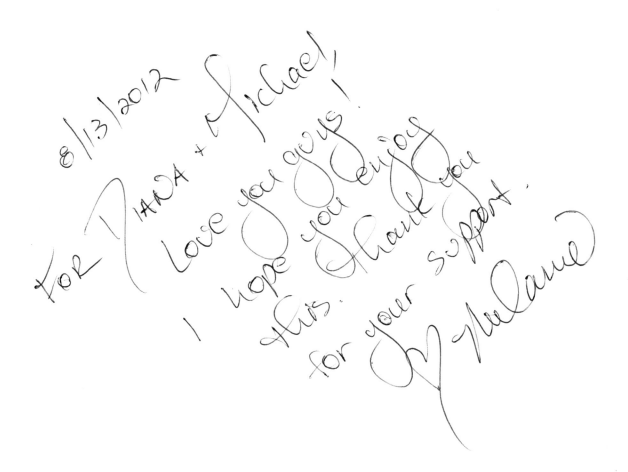

8/13/2012
For Diana + Michael,
Love you guys!
I hope you enjoy this. Thank you
for your support,
♡ Melanie

Copyright and Legal Information:

The Home Farming Revolution for Drylands

The Home Farming Revolution for Drylands
Table of Contents

Introduction

In this section you'll learn how this book developed from a partnership between Zoe Wilcox and Melanie Rubin, which in turn was connected to a community-based effort in Albuquerque, New Mexico to revolutionize how communities feed themselves. You'll get a sense of the many people who have been focused on this work for a long time in Albuquerque, as well as the support we received as we went through the process of developing the book. And you'll review some tips on how you can gain the most out of this book as you read through. Finally, you will consider some of the truly wonderful, as well as a few of the current-reality-based reasons, for home-farming.

Photograph by Sandra Pederson Hense

Dedication and Acknowledgements

This e-book is dedicated to the many people who are working to create access to healthy food for everyone.

First and foremost, we would like to thank Bard Edrington for his help and support in developing all aspects of this book, including, workshops, writing, editing, photography, and drawings.

Thank you as well to: Dr. Gary Moses, for his mentoring, and for contributing a great deal of his time in co-developing the bee chapter; Alison Yahna for her bee mentoring in Hawaii; Judith Phillips, author of *New Mexico Gardener's Guide* and other books, for reviewing the manuscript to provide her expert input and help us clarify a number of points; Nate Downey, author of *Harvest the Rain*, for reviewing the book; Jim Brookes, for giving us a great deal of valuable information, and donating truckloads of materials for the creation of Melanie's home farm; Joran Viers, for editing the chicken chapter; Kathleen Connors and Kim Blueher, for giving us excellent input and guidance as "non-expert" reviewers; and Kay Bird, who did a fabulous job as a copy-editor. We would like to thank Dr. Jay Polmar, Liliana Gonzalez Garcia, John Peragine, and their team at SpeedReadAmerica for their help in designing the book and mentoring us through the e-book and print-on-demand production processes.

Thank you to Gretchen Beaubier, Jessie Brown, Daniel Jaecks, Sharon Austin, Bob Morgan, Frances Deters, Lora Roberts, Carol Bennett, Steve and Mary Dorch, Susie Biggs, Charles Gallagher, Gina Ortiz, Jennifer Coston, Peg and Charlie Galbraith, and Sandra Pederson Hense who contributed photographs for this book.

Thanks as well to Marsha Keith and Carol Frappier for help developing the drawings. A special thank you to Tracey Fedor who finalized many of the drawings in this book.

We would like to thank everyone who, by attending and supporting our workshops at Mother Nature Gardens and Albuquerque Backyard Farms, helped us to develop much of the information that went into this book. Thanks are due in particular to our friends and colleagues who helped with assistance and promotion for these workshops, especially Pamela Heater, Gretchen Beaubier, Patricia Ames, Jane Craford, and Sharyn Franklin, and including:

Suzanne Dillon; Steve Glass; Eliseo Torres of UNM; Deborah Wakshull; Wally Lopez; Shane Harley; Ken Hatfield; Zaida Amaral; and Denis Doyon. We would also like to thank all the people who partnered with us to put on the workshops, including Yvonne Scott, Alberto Lopez, Casey Paul, Loralee Makela, Jessie Brown, Dr. Gary Moses, Jeff Parks, Lora Roberts, Suzanne Maxwell, Chery Klairwator, Jim Brookes, Rebecca Martin, Gretchen Beaubier, and Will Becktell. We would like to thank our sponsors who supported the early workshops in the Albuquerque Backyard Farms workshop series: Bruce Milne, Maggie Seeley, and Terry Horger of the UNM Sustainability Studies Department; Aldo Leopold Centennial Celebration; Soilutions; Rehm's Nursery; Kelly Koepke Professional Writing Services; Kyle Zimmerman Photography; The Source; Whole Foods; Seeds of Change; the Construction Department, City of Albuquerque; and Dion's Pizza. We would also like to thank our colleagues who helped us get the word out about this book, including Kate Manchester at Edible Santa Fe; Ann Simon and Lora Roberts at the MRCOG Agricultural Collaborative (and for giving us a place to meet in the first place); Wyatt Wegrzyn and Amy Lahti of Bookworks in Albuquerque; Maggie Seeley, Terry Horger, and Jessica Rowland of the UNM Sustainability Studies Department; and Robin Seidel of La Montanita Coop. Thank you to the Albuquerque Journal and Amanda Schoenberg for including us in reporting on Edible Landscaping.

We would like to give a special thank you to photographer Kyle Zimmerman, kylezimmermanphotography.com, for the cover and promotional photography, and for her design work on the front and back covers. Many thanks are due to Kyle as well for her practical support in getting the Home Farming Revolution web site launched, and helping Melanie with the online and social media aspects of delivering this message.

Last but not least, we would like to thank our family, friends, and colleagues who have together given us a great deal of moral and practical support at various stages throughout this process, and been patient with the trials and tribulations of getting this book into a form for distribution, including Isabelle Rubin-Labelle, Josh Rubin, Sandra Koehler, Cheyenne Maloney, Charles McCall, Pamela Heater, Yvonne Scott, James Rolwing, Kyle Zimmerman, Shane Harley, Larry Krizan, Nanette Redmond, Susan Greenfield, Gretchen Beaubier, Patricia Ames, Maggie Seeley, Lora Roberts, Michael Hyde, Steve Melby, Chery Klairwator, Robert Fowlie, Katya Miller, Bert Goodrich, Karen Stroker, Sherry Geyer, Larry Donahue, Ellen LaPenna, and Craig LeCompte.

About the Authors, and the Origins of this Book

About Zoe Wilcox

Farm-raised by two veterinarians in rural Illinois, I've always lived close to agriculture. In 2001, however, Australia introduced me to an approach to growing food unknown in my home region: Permaculture. I spent five months learning about Permaculture in Australia, with formal study at Crystal Water Permaculture Village. Slowly, Permaculture grew into everything I did.

Permaculture is a study of design that takes elements within a system and begins to interconnect them so that every element performs many functions and every function serves many elements. Another way to put it is that Permaculture is the study of how things connect and how to improve those connections. Although this is not a Permaculture book, it incorporates a great deal of Permaculture wisdom.

From 2003 to 2005, my husband, Bard Edrington, and I worked in Zambia, Africa with the US Peace Corps, living in a village hut with no running water, electricity, or motorized vehicles for 30 miles. The first year, we taught sustainable fish farming to villagers. The second year, I committed completely to researching alternatives to the widespread practice of slash-and-burn agriculture. I developed and taught a two-day workshop in alternative agricultural techniques that was hosted in a dozen villages before my departure. I then wrote the Peace Corps curriculum on sustainable agriculture for all agriculture volunteers coming into the country so that the work of educating self-sustaining farmers would easily continue. This book is deeply rooted in my work and writing in Zambia.

Upon our return to the states, my husband and I moved to Albuquerque. I began working almost immediately for Soilutions, Inc., a company that composts organic matter to create wonderful soil and mulching materials for gardens, landscapes, and farms. I continued to mentor under the owner and long-time drylands Permaculture expert Jim Brookes for two years. I am grateful for his knowledge, sprinkled throughout this book. Since 2009, I have partnered with Bard to run Mother Nature Gardens, a demonstration urban farm and learning center with tours, classes, and courses. I also help Bard manage Living Edge Landscaping, a sustainable and edible landscaping company based in Albuquerque, New Mexico (livingedgelandscaping.com). My development as a Permaculturist has always been side-by-side with Bard.

A Synchronistic Meeting

In the spring of 2009, I met Melanie Rubin, who had a dream of learning backyard farming, and teaching this work at her home in the city. She excelled at marketing and business strategies (something I had zero background in), but did not know the first thing about farming. We quickly saw how we could help each other and became partners. We began a workshop series at her home under the banner of "Albuquerque Backyard Farms," transforming her garden publicly, in bite-sized pieces, into a home farm. The workshops helped to formulate our ideas and Melanie's home farm, Sacred Heart Backyard Farm, as well as Mother Nature Gardens, are used as examples throughout this book. We will also refer to other home farms and edible landscapes Bard and I have helped to develop throughout Albuquerque.

Photograph I.1 Sacred Heart Backyard Farm, Photo by Gretchen Beaubier

About Melanie Rubin

Health has always been a passion for me, and I have provided business support for complementary health workers like naturopaths, chiropractors and acupuncturists for many years. My educational and professional background is in training development and delivery, curriculum design, project management, marketing and PR, video production, writing, and small business management and coaching.

In the fall of 2008, as I was waking up one morning, something seemed to whisper in my ear that it was time for me to work more specifically with food. I was the director of a bodywork school, with a focus on healing and keeping people healthy. "But," said the little voice in my ear, "if people don't have good food to eat, how healthy can we support them in being?" Suddenly my focus reoriented toward how I could help people become empowered to grow their own healthy food.

The problem was that I knew very little about how to grow food – and I knew I needed a partner.

Almost immediately the universe brought me into contact with Zoe Wilcox. I was sitting in at a meeting of Albuquerque's Mid-Region Council of Government's Agricultural Collaborative. When participants introduced themselves, my ears perked up like a rabbit's when Zoe introduced herself and Mother Nature Gardens. After the meeting, I nabbed her on the way out, introduced myself, and asked whether we could meet. Immediately, a new venture was launched. Although I had very little practical experience growing food, I did have a 50- by 50-foot backyard with nothing in it but weeds and dirt. We decided my garden and I would make a pretty good test case. Could I learn to grow a reasonable amount of healthy food at my home over the course of two or three years? We set about creating a workshop series that would teach me, and other people like me, what we needed to know.

About Contributing Authors

Because we wanted the knowledge in this book to be both broad and thorough, we collaborated with a number of experts along the way. You may already have gotten a feel for this by reading our acknowledgements. Permaculturist Bard Edrington provided many pictures of his work and contributed greatly to the information on outdoor living spaces and rainwater harvesting. Permaculturist Jim Brookes influenced a lot of the information in the book as well, particularly in the sections about rainwater harvesting. Third-generation beekeeper and naturopathic doctor, Dr. Gary Moses, worked step-by-step with Melanie to create the chapter on beekeeping.

Preface

About this Book

Developed out of our workshop series, this is a step-by step guide to help you convert any plot of land into a micro-farm. The book is written in Zoe's voice since she did most of the initial research and writing. Melanie helped to structure the material, added exercises and images, edited, and added stories from her home farm. As a newcomer to home farming, her experience shows that you do not need be an expert to become a home farmer. She also helped structure, complete, and market the book. Both Zoe and Melanie worked with contributing subject matter experts for certain chapters.

Tips for Using this Book

We hope this book will give you techniques and tools that will be very easy for you to apply on the property where you plan to do your home farming. As such, we've included a series of exercises to assist you in applying the concepts to your particular situation. You will get a lot more out of this book if you do the exercises.

We recommend that you keep paper and pencil on hand, and perhaps a notebook to store the site plans, sketches, and notes you will generate as you go through this book.

Although our homes are in the high drylands of New Mexico, the concepts presented in this book can be applied throughout the United States and beyond. Although we focus quite a bit on water harvesting and irrigation – inspired by the requirements of our dry climate – you don't need to be a desert rat to understand the importance of water conservation. In fact, changing weather patterns have caused severe droughts recently that have devastated former wetland locations. Fresh water is precious everywhere, and the people that capture and conserve it contribute to our global community's sustainability and their own peace of mind.

This book is divided into four sections that build on each other.

Section One, The Design, teaches you how to create your farm design by dividing your process into three steps:

Step One: Connect with your land by studying what already exists;

Step Two: Consider what you want to include in your home farm, and then;

Step Three: Blend what's already there with what you want to add in a functional and harmonious design using several design principles and techniques.

These are the first three chapters of the book. As you journey through the design process, you will experience several benefits:

- *You will develop a vision.* The ideal design probably won't strike like a lightning bolt as you stand in your yard, arms up, "connecting." Let it develop over time and trust your own intuition to get to know your land.

- *You will eliminate mistakes.* Wise planning saves time, money, and labor. We should all practice it. Borrow your farming wisdom from this book, neighbors who garden, and local gardening organizations.

- *You will become teachable.* Stewards of the land are students of the land. Good site assessment, which leads to a good design, depends on good listening. Have reverence for the tiny piece of Mother Earth with which you have been gifted and know that She has so much to teach you. Be open and responsive.

Section Two addresses the farm structures and systems that need to be implemented as part of your home farm. Ideally this structural part of the plan should be put in place early in the transformation process because it creates the skeleton that supports the living garden. Once human spaces are identified and water has been planned, it's time for the green stuff.

Section Three discusses food forests, building soil for veggie gardens, and how and when to plant them.

Section Four diversifies and interconnects your food production with information on raising chickens and taking care of honeybees.

Why Create a Home Farm

Photograph I.2 Everyone Loves Beautiful, Healthy Food!

Health Benefits of Eating Home Farming Produce

The benefits of creating home farms in our towns and cities are as plentiful as the bounty they produce. We need healthy food in order to be healthy! Our country faces a growing number of health concerns ranging from degenerative illnesses, such as diabetes, cancer, and heart disease, to mental and emotional conditions, such as attention-deficit disorder, depression, and severe anxiety. These illnesses are often catalyzed or exaggerated by poor nutrition in this, the "wealthiest nation in the world." Obesity among adults and children is also rampant, caused by too much of the wrong kind of food and not enough physical activity. Most Americans fill their grocery carts with food grown in unknown places and processed with unknown ingredients. Conventional grocery store foods are additive and calorie-rich, and nutrient-poor. Consumption of Genetically Modified Organism (GMO) foods, which are illegal in many countries, presents unknown long-term health concerns. Unless they are certified organic, fresh foods contain herbicides and pesticides.

Argentina, with its steep, forested slopes, grows many of our fruits, while Mexico, with its temperate winters and loose agro-chemical laws, grows many of our veggies. Machines or workers pick the fruits and vegetables when they are hard and green. Nutritional value deteriorates during weeks of transport and storage, which in itself takes massive amounts of fossil fuel. So even when food is certified organic, there is no assurance of freshness or high nutrient value. In addition, fresh fruits and vegetables cost much more than processed foods, creating a health-destructive cycle for low-income citizens. As gasoline prices continue to rise, the cost of produce grown far, far away will also increase.

We believe a person shouldn't have to be wealthy to eat healthy! Home farming provides healthy, organic food at peak freshness to all people despite economic status or location. Many unused plots of land in the city, suburbs, and country are just waiting to be used to grow produce. If we coordinate efforts, there can be land for everyone to farm, whether or not each person owns a home, or has a yard of his or her own. There are many models now of community gardens where people share land, resources, and knowledge to grow more food for everyone.

Photograph 1.3 Melanie with Tomatoes in her Garden, Photo by Gretchen Beaubier

Environmental and Health Impacts of Large Agribusiness

We believe our society needs to address other considerations when we talk about our current food system. When commercial farmers grow food in mono-crops laden with chemicals, this agricultural practice affects more than just the consumer – it also impacts field workers, wildlife from the area, the water systems, and the earth itself.

A Story from Zoe and Bard

When driving through Mexico recently, my family and I passed through Sinaloa, the state that grows most of our American grocery store produce. We saw seas of mono-crop vegetable production – tomatoes, cauliflower, carrots – that extended beyond the horizon. Crop duster planes swarmed the sky, dropping clouds of chemicals on the plants, while field workers fell in directly behind them to work. We kept the windows rolled up to avoid the air's acrid stench as we sped through the state to get away – and felt more fortunate than those living and raising families there. The toxic chemicals applied to produce growing in the fields are water-soluble and absorb quickly into the field workers' skin every time they touch a plant or the soil. Later, we learned that Sinaloa has record rates of cancer amongst young men in Mexico.

Photograph 1.4 Agricultural Chemical Plane Commonly Seen in Sinaloa, Mexico

As for the impact that mega-farming can have on local wildlife, Salinas Valley, California, which produces most of the world's lettuce, is a poignant example. Large commercial farming interests in valleys greatly affect wildlife populations by putting up fences that block passage between mountain ranges. Huge, uncovered fields with lots of human activity and noisy tractors dominate the ecosystem. However, things got worse for local wildlife of Salinas Valley following an e coli breakout. Farmers falsely blamed wildlife for the spread of the disease. Agribusiness companies began erecting fences around the fields, making them completely impassible for wildlife. Along the fence line, company workers placed thousands of poisoning stations, upside down T's made of PVC piping that distribute poisonous pellets. Rodents got to the poison first, but raccoons, skunks, and possum also ate it. Then, everything that ate those animals ingested the poison: owls, eagles, hawks, coyotes, bobcats, etc. Before conscious and informed citizens could organize against these practices, the entire food chain of the area had been tragically affected.

Of course, the water system and the Earth itself also suffer from our current food production system. The water absorbs field toxins and spreads them to other places, including underground water supplies. River systems show signs of disease with toxic buildup. The Earth continues to absorb the poisons flushed through it like a liver in the body of an alcoholic. If the production of food, which gives us life, creates so much death, we need a revolutionary change to our food production system. Home farming inaugurates that revolution slowly and subtly, one balcony, yard, and empty lot at a time. In addition to the direct benefits they offer, home farms lower our dependence on "anti-life" food production systems.

Other Benefits of Home Farming

Sustainable farms are renewable, cyclical, and self-cleansing. As organisms live and die in a home farm, death is quickly transformed into more life of another variety. Creating a recycling system like this on our little plot of land not only minimizes waste, it grounds and calms us as we witness that no death or destruction is permanent in nature but is only a gateway to rebirth and renewal. This is a lesson that is especially important for children.

Home farming requires regular physical activity, another selling point. The gentle, daily exercise of moving about our yard – feeding, harvesting, planting, and maintaining – strengthens our bodies and increases vitality. In addition to stronger bodies, we create stronger communities. With time spent in our yards, we become part of the environment, increasing our chances to connect and share with our neighbors.

Photograph I.5 Zoe Demonstrates that Home Farming is Great Exercise

Farming, even in the city, requires that we reconnect with nature. We will elaborate on this point throughout this book because of the powerful significance this reconnection has on our mental and emotional lives. Becoming aware of our natural surroundings and listening to nature is our starting point in this long journey. While we work in our yards, we notice migrating birds and other wildlife, and appreciate the coming and going of each season. Our work changes with the activities of the season, and after a few years we start to really understand the rhythm and renewal we help create. Putting our hands in the dirt heals our souls, and seeing the life that springs up from that dirt gives us peaceful reassurance that something greater than we are is providing for us. In fact, the Earth is responsible for gathering spent life and transforming it into new life. Natural habitats stay fertile because leaves fall each autumn, animals and bugs die continuously, and the Earth decomposes those things into fertile soil from which new life can emerge. The Earth has the same effect on us every time we touch it. Transforming bare soil or cement patios into growing gardens transforms us.

Photograph I.6 Zoe and Bard's Son in the Garden

All the souls and human bodies that need healing in our communities make a perfect match for all the land waiting to be healed. Gardens bring comfort to the elderly, help restore patients with mental illnesses, and are used as a form of therapy in jails.

Children seem especially calmed and healthy when they spend a lot of time outdoors. That bond strengthens and forms a web of nourishment and connection when our children experience the outdoors with adults. Home farms provide huge opportunities to interact and learn with our children in positive ways. We can build together, observe how life evolves, and attune ourselves to the cycles of the moon and the seasons.

Home farming also provides us with many of the things we need to thrive when other economic and food systems in our society fall short. Moving food from place to place requires a tremendous amount of energy, currently in fossil fuel resources, as does driving to the store to buy our food. When we grow food at home, we conserve fossil fuel resources. This is one of the many reasons why so many people are now advocating the importance of growing food locally. As the door shuts on one system, we can choose to open the door on another healthier, whole, and connected system.

As professional landscapers, my husband Bard Edrington and I spend a lot of time pulling back plastic weed barriers and rock from hot and barren southwest yards. The trees that poke themselves up from under that plastic barrier and rock have incredibly shallow root systems packed mostly into the top four to six inches of soil. Because of the plastic barrier, they have been cut off, disconnected from air and water, and they desperately search for these basic sources of life. This makes the trees extremely vulnerable to two dangers. In dry times, a tree with a shallow root system can't tap into deep sources of water and thus can perish from thirst. In high winds, a tree with a shallow root system is susceptible to toppling over because it is not well braced against the forces of the wind. By contrast, in hard times trees that are deeply rooted in the earth survive. As students of nature, we need to heed this warning. We need to pull back the "plastic barrier" that separates us from our connection with the Earth and dig in our roots. In doing so, we will heal our little portion of the Earth and ourselves at the same time.

Living by Example with Zoe and Bard's Demonstration Farm, Mother Nature Gardens

Since Bard and I met in 2000, we have traveled through Australia, Africa, Mexico, and a half a dozen states within the United States working with people who practice sustainability. We've invested a great deal of labor into other people's dreams for sustainability, and we're grateful for the education these experiences have provided us. Through the years we spent on other people's land, we never stopped daydreaming about what we would do on our own place when we finally owned property. Rooted in our country upbringing, we created a wishful mantra about acquiring "our 5 to 10 acres in the country."

Reality hit, however, when we began to look into buying our country acreage and realized it was way beyond our financial means at the time. Eventually, in 2007, we bought what we could afford: a small home on an eighth of an acre, in a low-income and heavily drug trafficked neighborhood one block off the historic Route 66 in Albuquerque, New Mexico. When we visited the property before we bought it, somehow we didn't notice the traffic that passed 20 feet from the house, cars and trucks blaring a cultural cornucopia of music: mariachi, hip-hop, and heavy metal. We didn't see the raw street life to which our country-bumpkin eyes were unaccustomed, nor did we hear the chorus of pit bulls and Chihuahuas all around us. We saw a large city plot of barren, exhausted land and our hearts swelled with its potential.

In fact, we became obsessed with the possibility of creating as much life as possible in that little space. In the next three and a half years, we built a straw bale shed, a 2,900-gallon rainwater cistern, shade structures, chicken houses, cold frames, an outdoor laundry and sink area with a greywater system, a play house, a home for honeybees, a food forest (which we will explain in Chapter Seven), and veggie beds. We have developed the soil so much that you can lose your elbow while digging for the original compact clay. Gracefully undulating garden beds produce food for us nine months out of the year and fill our freezer for the winter. Our food production thrives almost entirely on harvested rainwater so, despite our intensive home farming, we use less water per person than the city's average. Our chickens provide eggs for us, as well as an occasional feast of chicken and dumplings. Honeybees pollinate our flowers, fruit, and vegetable crops, and give us honey, medicine, and wax, which I use to produce candles for holiday gifts. As I prepare for winter, I gather and dry over a dozen medicinal herbs that I make into teas to help keep my family strong and healthy throughout the cold and flu season. We do not produce all of our food on the farm, but we produce enough that we can afford to select high quality, ethically-produced food when we do shop.

Photograph I.7 "Before" at Mother Nature Gardens, Facing West Away from the House

This abundance does not come from the five acres in the country we envisioned. It comes from an eighth of an acre in the heart of our beautiful city, which grows healthier every day with efforts like these. I can harvest eggs from the chickens for breakfast and eat them accompanied by home-remedy herbal tea sweetened with my own honey, and then walk two blocks to catch the city bus.

By starting where we were, we learned that you don't need acreage to farm. In fact, many times, we have expressed gratitude that we started our farming on a small property since we might have become overwhelmed with uncompleted projects on a larger plot of land. In our yard, we have learned to perfect efficiency and maximize production and have amazed ourselves with what you can grow in a relatively small space.

Photograph I.8 Rainwater Cistern Added at Mother Nature Gardens, Facing East Toward the House

Photograph I.9 "After" at Mother Nature Gardens, Facing West Away from the House

Revisiting a Different Way of Life

Our community has greatly improved in the last several years, and gardening is popular. As a former Spanish land trust area, our neighborhood includes many residents with a long lineage on this land. This part of the Rio Grande Valley once provided most of the food for the city. Many neighbors only have to go back a generation or two to find a family member who depended on growing their own food.

We hope to facilitate the movement back to that lifestyle in our area, where abundance comes from within the city (not imported from the outside), where every socio-economic class can enjoy the best and most healthy food available, and we can build community around farming anywhere there is even a small piece of land.

We hope you will enjoy this book, and that it will help and inspire you in your own journey toward health, abundance, raising delicious food at home, and contributing to the amazing beauty and bounty of life on this planet.

Your Notes

section 1
The Design

In the three chapters of The Design section, you will learn how to work with your property by connecting with it first and becoming a student of the land. Along the way, you will become aware of how you can develop an inspired vision for converting your property (whether it's a small or a large area) into an organic, somewhat self-sustaining, food-producing mini-farm.

Chapter One:

Connecting with Your Land

Design Step One: Connecting with Your Land Using the Four Earth Elements

 **Overview**

To connect with a piece of land we study what already exists. This is called *site assessment.* The first step to changing your land, or most anything else for that matter, is being present with it as it is. Consider what you are doing as "long and thoughtful observation." You may think that *nothing* is happening on your site. Yet even on barren ground, water falls, weeds grow, land rises and slopes, wind blows, and the soil below holds the land's history. The quality of your design depends on your thoroughness in assessing all the natural and man-made factors that create your site. You can't harvest water effectively if you don't understand how it moves on the land. You won't grow veggies as effectively if you don't know the path of the sun's rays across your vegetable bed, or the shade offered by the trees that are sharing the veggie bed's root space.

Practice this shift in perspective: if you were the land on your site, what would it feel like to be you? Imagine the land's condition at different times of the day, in wet times and in dry, in the heat and in the wind. Many elements can affect the land's state. So, we give structure to this assessment process by considering the four earth elements, Water, Fire (the Sun), Air, and Earth, and how each of these earth elements affects the site.

 **Water**

We start with **Water** because it is the primary limiting factor for how much we can grow, especially in drylands. Where there is water, there is life. In arid lands, we want to harvest every bit of water that falls on our site, so we depress our growing beds, making them the low point in the land. In Step One of the design process, we observe how water falls on and moves over our land.

> ### Helpful Notes: Observing Water in Other Regions of the Country.
>
> First, identify how many inches of rain your area receives each year. When does the moisture generally come? Do you have wet seasons or is your moisture more continual? If you have gardened before, when during the gardening season does supplemental water become important? If you're not sure, do an Internet search or call your librarian and ask him or her for help determining how much rain your area receives month-by-month. How have recent changes in weather patterns affected your area? If those weather pattern changes continue, how will they affect the process of growing food in your area?

Begin at the Top

Once you have an idea of how much moisture you're getting and when you get it, find the top of your watershed. This is where water enters your property. For most urban properties, the top of the watershed is the roof of the house or residence. If your land slopes, water also enters at the high point of the slope. Water may also enter your property from street run-off, sidewalks, or neighbors' gutters.

Once you know where the water comes from, where does it go? Does it puddle in certain places or flow over the land? Ideally, you will watch where storm water flows during a storm. This will tell you the water's pathway by firsthand observation. If you miss the storm, you can use detective-like observation to piece together the story. Where does land stay wet the longest? Have drip lines formed depressions anywhere on the land, beneath awnings, gutters, or trees? Has mud splattered against the house or garage walls suggesting water buildup below? Where are pioneer tree species (the first plant arrivals on untended land) and weeds sprouting up? They indicate extra water in the soil. Finally, where does water leave your property? What are the low points of the land?

Look at Supplemental Supply

Now, look at your supplemental supply of water. Are you on well water or city water? Where are the hose spigots? Do you currently have an irrigation system and if so, how effective is it?

Because water is imperative for life, and it's so important to protect our fresh water supply, we have included a whole chapter on the topic of sustainable watering, chapter five. This section is only an observational introduction. It is possible to find all the water you need to grow a lot of food on your lot – big, small, or in containers – without relying on scarce and dwindling aquifer or river water. We can maximize our use of the water that falls on our property by gathering it in condensed growing areas.

There are four possible sources of water in any garden system:

1. **Passive rainwater harvesting.** Passive rainwater harvesting captures, slows, and moves water across your land through the use of earthworks, i.e. shaping the earth to direct the flow of water or keep it where you want it to stay. Earthworks change the shape of the land to direct storm water deliberately to where you need it and away from areas where you don't want it. The goal is to keep 100% of the water that falls on the property and to store it in the earth where it benefits life, and not on the surface of the soil where it causes erosion and damages building foundations.

2. **Active rainwater harvesting.** This means catching water runoff from roofs, ideally, in a large capacity cistern, i.e. a tank that can hold hundreds or thousands of gallons of rainwater. We harvest rainwater during wet periods for redistribution during dry periods.

3. **Greywater.** Greywater is water that has been used once (like for washing clothes or dishes), and is then used again for your garden.

4. **Hose tap.** In chapter six, we will discuss drip irrigation systems that distribute our well and city water, as well as rainwater, as efficiently as possible.

Photograph 1.1 Water Sources - Passive Rainwater Harvesting

Photograph 1.2 Water Sources - Active Rainwater Harvesting

Photograph 1.3 Water Sources - Greywater Systems

1.1

1.2

1.3

 Fire

Overview

The second earth element is **Fire.** Here, we look at how the sun travels over your property at different times of the year. We study its effects on your home and farm elements. We discuss how to shade farm elements properly when they receive a surplus of sun and welcome sun where there's a lack of it. We consider wildfires and give elementary tips on how to protect your home from them, if they are a concern in your neighborhood.

A home's relationship to the sun affects its temperature fluctuations dramatically. Paying attention to the sun's movements allows us to maximize its heating benefits in the winter and protect ourselves from its intensity in the summer. Read this section before you buy solar paneling to meet your home's energy needs. Proper landscaping can greatly reduce cooling and heating costs. At Mother Nature Gardens, we have cut off months of swamp cooler use (an alternative to an air conditioner in the south west), in the summer and fall by removing gravel around the house, and adding shade structures and well-placed trees.

> ### Helpful Notes: Sun Considerations in Regions Other Than the Southwest
>
> Sun shines differently in different parts of the US. In the Southwest, our concern is usually receiving too much sun, i.e. having too much "solar gain." In other areas of the country the challenge may be not having enough sun, or not enough "solar gain." A plant that thrives in "full sun" in the Midwest can perish from full sun in the Southwest. So become familiar with the solar gain considerations in your region. If the home farming potential where you live is negatively affected by deep shade, this section will offer tips on where to open up your canopy for best solar gain in your garden.

Observe the Movement of the Sun

Let's begin by observing the movements of the sun. In the winter, the sun rises in the southeast. It is at its southern-most point in the sky of the northern hemisphere on December 21ˢᵗ. Each day it follows a short, low arch across the sky, casting mild, horizontal light onto the northern hemisphere. Then, it sets in the southwestern sky. The winter sun warms and lights our days and helps to lessen the impact of the long, cold nights. This is the time of the year when we want to welcome this gentle, low-light sun into our homes as much as possible, with clear, south-facing windows.

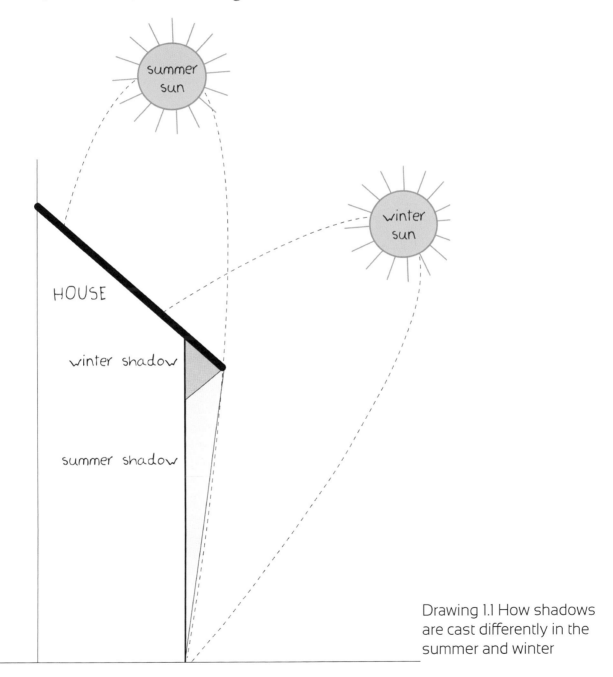

Drawing 1.1 How shadows are cast differently in the summer and winter

At the opposite end of the calendar is June 21ˢᵗ, the summer solstice, when the sun follows its longest arch across the sky. After December 21ˢᵗ the sun moves farther and farther north in our sky, increasing the length of each day, until June 21ˢᵗ when it rises north of due east. On that date, it follows a long, tall arch across the sky and sets north of due west. To live comfortably and sustainably, we must protect our homes from this fierce summer sun. During this time of the year, the sun's morning light beams against the eastern walls of our homes all morning long. Then, the sun beams against the western wall all afternoon long. In the Southwest, these areas typically need shade provided by trees and shade structures to prevent our homes from acting like solar ovens. In addition to whatever other benefits our landscapes give us, they should also passively control our indoor temperatures.

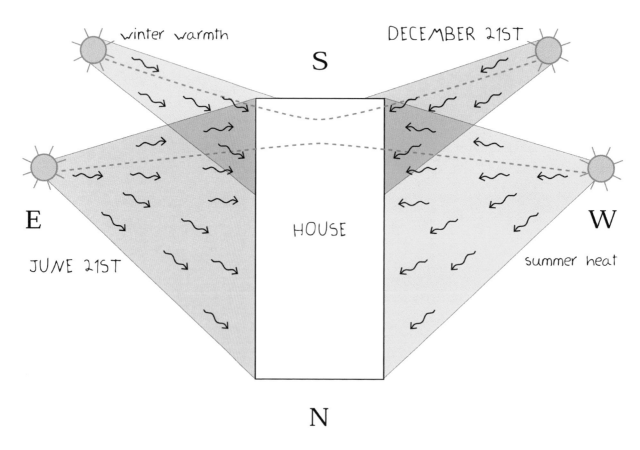

Drawing 1.2 How summer and winter sun warms a house built along an east-west axis

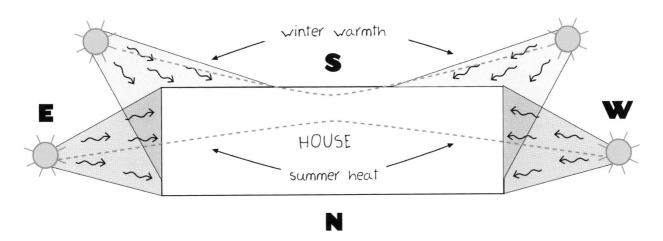

Drawing 1.3 How summer and winter sun warms a house built along a east-west axis

 Exercise 1.1 The Fire Element on Your Property

1. Use a plot plan for your house, or sketch an outline of your house on your property, including the location of all of the windows.

2. Find the cardinal directions in relation to your house and add these to your drawing. A compass helps tremendously in this process. Tall buildings surrounding a property or properties that aren't on a grid can deceive the observer without a compass confirmation. Does the house sit on an east/west axis or a north/south axis? (Homes and buildings with a long north/south axis have more exposure to summer's morning and afternoon sun, thereby making them much hotter inside in the summer. Their lack of southern exposure makes them colder in the winter.)

3. What is the sun's path in the winter and in the summer across the property? Mark this on your drawing. Make sure to include where the sun rises and sets on the winter and summer solstices. This will be four separate locations. You will end up with a drawing something like 1.2 or 1.3 above.

4. Highlight the windows on the east and west side of the house. Do they have protection from the sun? Is the south side of the house open to allow winter light to shine in the house? If so, note this on your drawing.

5. Are there hot spots in your yard? How can they be cooled? Note this on your drawing.

Our Home Farms
From Melanie

Melanie's backyard has a southeastern exposure, with some large trees overhead, but in general, a lot of sun. In fact, we realized that protection from the sun would be an important consideration while plants were getting established. As well, we saw that we would need to watch the intensity of the afternoon sun in the summer beaming into the chicken coop, and provide extra shade in that area during that portion of the year. We also realized additional shade protection was needed in the outdoor living space during the summer, so we planned for and installed a simple shade sail, a type of cloth that is very resilient to solar radiation, and can be used in place of a more structural roof, overhang, or portico. To see examples, go to hayneedle.com and search "shade sail."

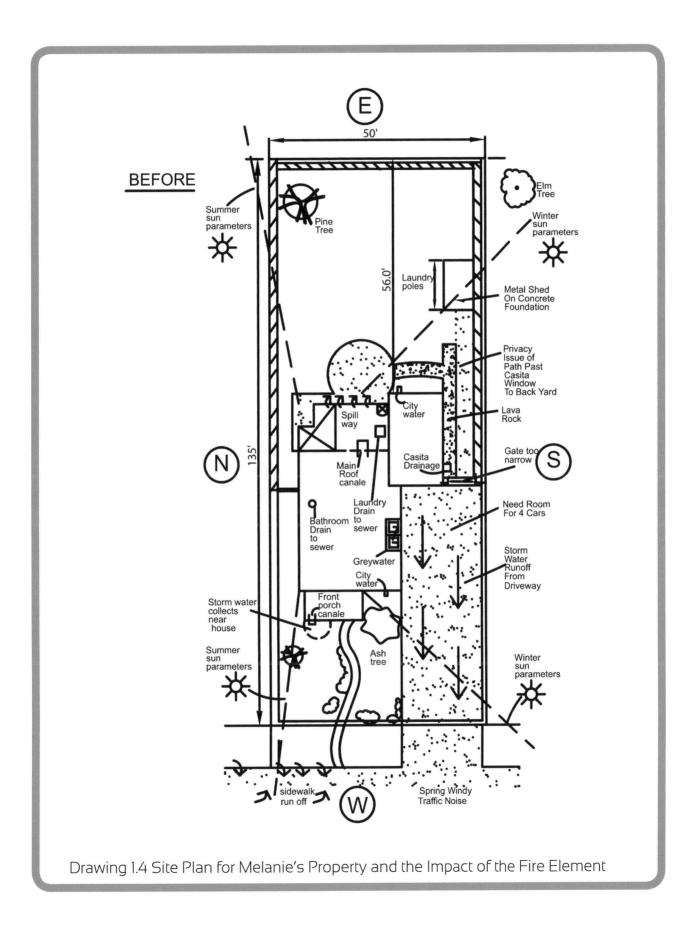

Drawing 1.4 Site Plan for Melanie's Property and the Impact of the Fire Element

Solar Tree Arch

A solar tree arch is a ring of trees and shrubs that wraps around the north side of a home and extends to the east side and west side like arms. It maximizes the benefits and minimizes the detriments of sun for a home. This arc of foliage remains open from the southeast to the southwest, welcoming the gentle winter light. In the east, trees block the home from morning sun in the summer, keeping the indoor temperatures cooler longer. The trees on the northern side protect the home from northern winter winds, insulating the home, while the trees on the western side shield the home from afternoon sun in the summer, which is the hottest part of the day during the hottest part of the year.

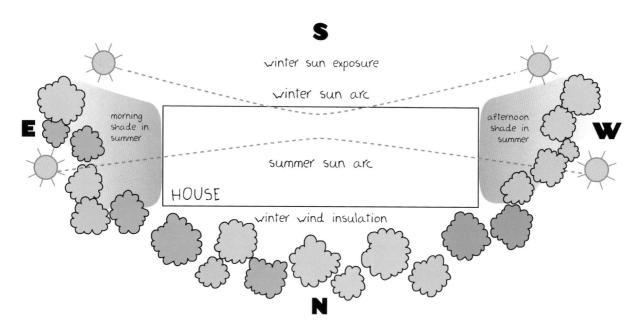

Drawing 1.5 Solar Tree Arch

Photograph 1.4 The West-facing Porch at Mother Nature Gardens

Not all properties or designs will allow for the full ring of trees in a solar tree arch. You can use shade structures in addition to or instead of trees and shrubs with the same effect. Use this design idea as a tool that you can adapt to your unique site. It will help you incorporate passive solar heating and cooling as you plan your home farm.

Plants and animals need the same attention, using the same design principles, to meet a balanced sun-diet. As much as plants and animals need sun, they also need protection from the sun. So, when we consider fire, or sun, on our property, we must think about where shade may be needed for every element in our home farm.

Wildfires

Wildfires are not a concern for a lot of urban dwellers, but when they are a concern, it is a serious one. If wildfires may be an issue in your area, know where prevailing winds come from since they will carry the fire. You can help to slow and divert fires with high-water-content plants located in a windbreak that runs perpendicular to the direction of prevailing winds. (You will learn more about windbreaks in Chapter Seven: Food Forests.) Moist beds and screened-in porches around the house, particularly on the windward side of the house, will further protect the home in case of fire. If you have the good luck to be able to choose your house location when building your home, avoid locating your home on a ridge if possible, since heat creates updrafts and ridges attract the hottest fires.

 Exercise 1.2 Using Landscaping Elements to Protect Your Home from the Fire Element

1. Review the notes you made on your site plan in Exercise 1.1, including which windows may need protection during the summer, whether the south side of your home in general may need protection during the summer, and where there may be hot spots in your yard.

2. Identify where you might want sun-protecting foliage in the summer in the east, west, and south.

3. Identify where you might want wind-protecting foliage in the winter in the north and west.

4. Identify any other needs for changing existing landscaping to minimize solar gain during the summer, and maximize solar gain during the winter.

5. Do wildfires pose much threat to your home? If so, how will you incorporate fire protection in your design?

 **Air**

Overview

As you connect with your property and the Earth element Air, notice the air quality, wind, noise, and views. Urban air carries many pollutants. Transforming your yard into a thriving ecosystem gradually helps to filter many of these pollutants out of the air. In the meantime, you can work toward creating more still, peaceful conditions in your garden. To grow the most food possible on your site, and enjoy the property to its fullest, you will want to block wind, filter noise and other pollutants, and deliberately direct your views. Wind severely stresses young plants and lowers their success rate, while what you look at powerfully impacts how you feel. We consider all these questions with the Earth element, Air.

Wind & Windbreaks

At my home, we experience brutal spring winds from the west. When does wind affect your property and from what direction does it come? Wind, like most things, has advantages and disadvantages. Light winds cool houses and people. They disperse pollen and seed, clear pollution, and aerate ponds. Hot winds in summer, however, can overheat a house and remove humidity while cold winds in winter suck the heat out of a home. Winds dry out and erode soil, strip needed moisture from around plant leaves, and stress the cells of the plants. Wind has the same effect on us and on our pets as it does on plants, drying and stressing our systems. Orchard yields can be destroyed by very hot or very cold winds during flowering. The life we cultivate and host on our farms, including chickens, bees, dogs, plants, and ourselves, needs protection from these harsh winds. By observing what type of winds move across your property and in what direction, you will be able to design for more stillness on your property.

If you experience heavy winds, whether they are too hot or too cold or too dusty, you may want to include a windbreak as part of your design. An ideal windbreak is not solid but allows 40% of the wind to pass through. Solid windbreaks, such as a wall or an evergreen hedge, create wind eddies which can be more destructive than the original wind flow. Alternating wood slat fences, coyote fences (young pine or aspen poles wired side by side), wire mesh, and deciduous hedges and trees (which can be intermixed with pines), make good windbreaks.

Plant your windbreak perpendicular to the direction of prevailing winds in a zigzag formation versus a straight line. The zigzag prevents wind from tunneling between the mature trees of your windbreak. You also want the wind to hit low shrubs first and then higher trees for a logical lift instead of tunneling. A proper windbreak will block wind six times the distance of the height of the windbreak. For example, a 10-foot high windbreak will block wind for 60 feet behind the windbreak. So know the height of the trees you wish to plant and then multiply that by 6 and you have your range of the area behind it that the windbreak will protect. An ideal windbreak extends 50 feet wider than the area you are blocking as wind will eddy around the ends of the windbreak. For example, if the width of the area you want to protect is 50 feet wide, ideally your windbreak would be 100 feet wide. So, a windbreak that is 10 feet tall and 100 feet wide would protect an area behind it that is 60 feet deep by 50 feet wide.

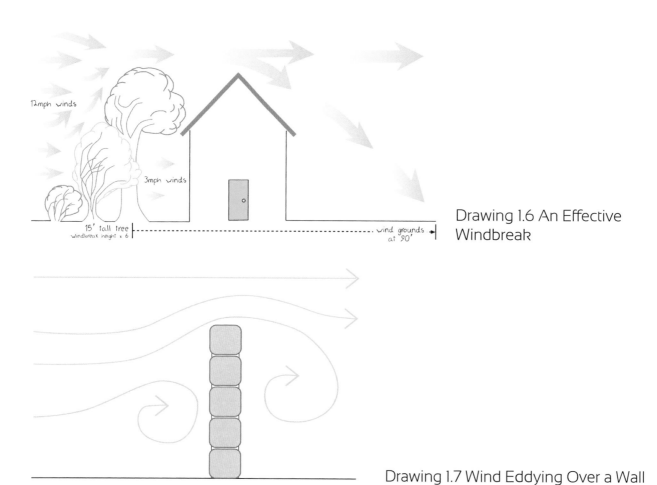

Drawing 1.6 An Effective Windbreak

Drawing 1.7 Wind Eddying Over a Wall

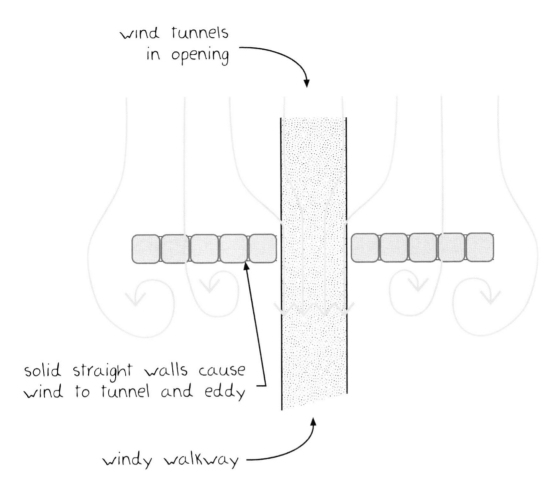

wind tunnels
in opening

solid straight walls cause
wind to tunnel and eddy

windy walkway

Drawing 1.8 Windy Walkway

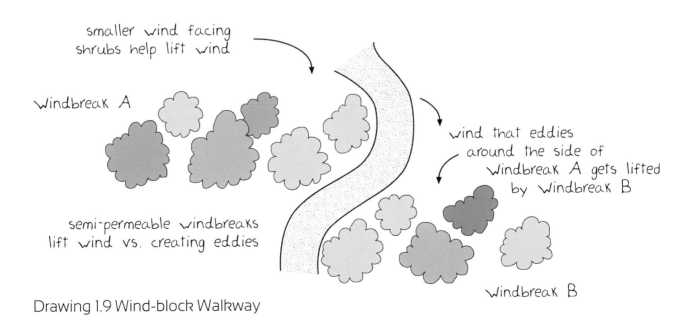

smaller wind facing
shrubs help lift wind

Windbreak A

wind that eddies
around the side of
Windbreak A gets lifted
by Windbreak B

semi-permeable windbreaks
lift wind vs. creating eddies

Windbreak B

Drawing 1.9 Wind-block Walkway

If you are blocking spring winds, fruit trees are not ideal choices because the wind they block may destroy their blossoms. A few exceptions include mulberry, carob, and nut trees. You may also want to use species that are native to your area or nitrogen-fixing species like Siberian pea shrub and sea buckthorn. A windbreak should always consist of two to four varieties of species that have different growth rates so that you have quick fill as well as long-lasting fill. If you are on a small property, however, a non-food-producing windbreak may take up more space than you are willing to give up to non-food producers. In that case, your windbreak will need to double as a food forest (see Chapter Seven). You may also wish to incorporate a fence as part of the windbreak, as mentioned above. Also, use hardier food-producing trees, like apples and nut trees, to take most of the impact, while using more tender fruit trees, like pears and peaches, where there is more protection. One source for ordering fruit trees online is fast-growing-trees.com. This supplier has a page for each state in the U.S. which shows which trees grows best there. Windbreaks can also double as shade structures, privacy structures, and screens that block out unwanted views.

 Exercise 1.3 Use the Site Plan for Your Property that You Sketched Previously

1. Observe where winds come from at different times of the year. Don't have time to figure it out? Ask a neighbor who is outside often and see what he or she tells you.

2. Identify what you want to protect (the house, a walkway, the chicken run, etc.) and from which direction you want to provide protection.

3. Find out where to put the windbreak with respect to what's being protected, such as your house or sittitng area. If you had a 12-foot tall windbreak made of trees, it would lift wind a distance of 72 feet past the trees. Remember, wind eddies around the edges of a windbreak, so you want the windbreak to be 50 feet wider than the area you're protecting. Alternatively, you can make the first windbreak flow into

another windbreak. Where within the space you want to protect do you have the width to plant a windbreak?

4. Choose trees for your windbreak that are available, inexpensive, appropriate, and legal to purchase or grow in your area.   Make sure you have at least two different heights of trees. You can sometimes get free or at least good deals on natives trees at your local Department of Forestry.

5. Lay out your plants in a zigzag formation, with the shortest shrub being the first to meet the wind.

6. Then, follow the tree planting instructions in Chapter Seven.

Noise

Noise rides on the currents of air. In heavily populated environments or properties next to busy roads, there are often anxiety-causing noises, including sirens, traffic, and fireworks (this season lasts for months in our neighborhood). Planting **green fences,** i.e. fences made of living plants, absorbs sound in the prettiest way. However, lush green sound barriers can be slow to cultivate. We have become admirers of fences and walled courtyards since our days as urban citizens. They make great backdrops for maturing gardens. Coyote fences give a rustic feel while blocking sound and 90% of your view of the neighbors. If water is available, plant your fences with clinging vines to improve the effectiveness of the sound barrier. Undulating walls and fences seem to deflect sound and wind more effectively than straight walls and are more visually interesting.

Photograph 1.5 The Front Wall at Mother Nature Gardens with Passing Traffic

Views

As we've mentioned already in passing, also include views under the Air element. Consider what you do and do not want to look at when you work or rest in your garden, and to plan accordingly. We can transform eyesores on our own property to be more aesthetic, but we have less control of the world around us. It's important to keep beautiful views clear, and densely plant or fence areas that have annoying or disturbing views. Your preferences for views will greatly impact seating area placement. Walk around your space with a lawn chair. Sit in different spots on your property and notice what you see from where. You are creating your own Eden here, so your design should accentuate what makes you happy and disguise what doesn't.

Photograph 1.6 A Garden Patio with a View

Neighborhood Relations

As well, consider how your garden will allow you to relate to your neighbors and neighborhood. It is important to have privacy, with the ability to interact and connect. Most people don't want to see their neighbors during their private moments in their yard, but do want to have easy, over-the-fence type interactions. The level of interaction you want to allow for will depend, of course, on your personal preferences and individual situation.

Summary of Air Considerations

How the element Air affects your property will have important impacts on your design. Through proper observation during site assessment, you will design for a quieter garden that shields the living things in your environment from harsh winds and the noise of urban areas, and highlights what's most beautiful in your surroundings.

Our Home Farms
From Melanie

Melanie's backyard can get very breezy during the spring when the Albuquerque winds blow. However, the five-foot cinderblock wall that already existed around the garden before we began design helps to serve as a windbreak, and to create visual privacy, as well as protection from neighborhood animals.

She had one small view of the Sandia Mountains along the northeast corner of her yard, which was more evident in winter with minimal foliage on the trees, and less evident in summer. There was also a Ponderosa pine tree in this corner of the yard, and we trimmed the branches of that tree to optimize her view (an Air element issue).

When we located the chicken coop, we encountered a conflict with several needs related to site assessment. We wanted to take advantage of the shade under the pine tree with the positioning of the coop (a Fire element issue), as well as Melanie's ability to observe the chickens while she worked at her desk in her office (another Air element issue). Out of consideration for the neighbors' concern about odors in the coop (another Air element issue), we wanted to locate the coop far enough back on the property to allay their fears. We also wanted to create a coop that Melanie could walk into to clean and remove eggs. Melanie did not sufficiently observe the Air parameters of the situation before approving the location and height of the design, however, so the coop partially obscured her small view when it was installed. It is likely she will relocate the coop in the future to reveal more of the view once again. This is a good example of how more observation than you think necessary is a very good idea when planning your site! It also shows how designing your site is an evolutionary process.

Photograph 1.7 The Placement of Melanie's Chicken Coop in Her Yard Partially Obscures the View of the Mountains

 Earth

Finally, we look at the **Earth** element Earth by identifying existing structures, trees, cement, gravel, and soil on the property. Features that are part of this element are stable and slow to change. Their impact is huge but often subtle.

Existing Structures

Existing structures have several effects on the property. The home acts as the visual and resource centerpiece. All interaction with elements on our home farm must relate back to the home. It is the nucleus of our farm. Our house, garages, and sheds create destination points. It's important to connect all the existing structures with pathways in the design, so their locations impact the layout of our growing areas considerably. When first stepping onto a property, notice the paths that people and pets have worn into the ground between existing structures. They are the "paths of least resistance." Because we always revert to the paths of least resistance as garden dwellers, you must honor these in the design. If you have a dirt path in your yard from your house to your garage, that path should also be in your final design, built into the overall elegant, arching pathways.

See photographs 1.8 and 1.9 on the next page

Finally, because they cast shade, absorb heat, and shed water, existing structures create microclimates: hot sides, cooler sides, and wet areas. These also need to be taken into consideration when planning the layout of your garden beds.

Trees

Next in the Earth category, we look at trees. What's growing in your yard? What's doing well and what needs extra care? If a tree is struggling, evaluate whether it is a good choice for your climate. If this type of tree is generally successful in your area, but is not doing well on your property, what needs of this tree must you address in your design? Is it competing with other trees? Is it getting enough water? Are its roots being damaged?

Photograph 1.8 Zoe supervises construction of the paths for Melanie's home farm

Laying the path to the shed

Pavers mark the path

Photograph 1.9 Before design, pavers mark the path to Melanie's shed

All trees bring some benefits, but some prove more beneficial than others. Some trees also have certain detriments that make them best to phase out or eliminate from the start. Every climate has an invasive species to contend with like the eucalyptus in California, and the Siberian elm and tree of heaven in the Southwest. These pioneering species thrive on our abused and stripped land by being very aggressive and greedy for resources. They can actually lower water tables and strangle out native species. If you have an invasive tree thriving in your yard, evaluate how much it will compete with your new plantings versus how much benefit it is giving you in shade. This assessment will tell you whether or not to keep the tree. (NOTE: Learn to identify invasive species in your area by calling a county extension agent or local tree nursery.)

Some trees are allelopathic, like mulberry, juniper, tree of heaven, walnut, and eucalyptus. This means that they release a chemical into the soil through their roots or through the decomposition of their leaves that inhibits the development and growth of the plants around them. That doesn't mean we must cut down all these types of trees in our communities. It does mean, however, that we need to think carefully about the area beneath any of these trees and what we can do with that space.

While these trees are not ideal at sharing space with other plants, you can still appreciate their shade. So you might decide to put your patio and picnic table beneath them instead of your garden. When evaluating trees on your site, notice what's growing on your neighbors' properties. Allelopathic trees next door will also impact your soil since below the earth surface, roots do not obey our "property" boundaries.

Our Home Farms
From Zoe

A Siberian elm tree lives in the eastside of our yard. For two years, we could not get anything to grow beneath it. Yet, it provided so much morning shade on our home that it cooled it considerably during our blistering summers. So we decided to build a small patio and place the doghouse in its shade. We also placed our water fountain and a few hardy species there, and began experimenting with growing flowers and vegetables in planted pots. Thanks to this tree, I have learned that I love intermixing veggies and flowers in pots. Since these are close to my kitchen, I water them with the greywater collected in a tub in my kitchen sink.

Concrete and Gravel

When we consider the Earth element, we take note of all concrete and gravel located on the property. Large slabs of concrete and fields of gravel are obstacles to implementing many of the sustainability techniques we have described so far. Concrete not only renders the earth beneath it fairly lifeless, it increases reflective light, and heats up the area all around it.

Together, in very warm climates, these materials create the *heat island effect*. With the heat island effect, cement and gravel, along with homes and buildings, absorb the sun's rays all day long. When the sun goes down and the air temperature cools, these materials begin to re-radiate their absorbed heat back into the air. Tucson, Arizona and Las Vegas, Nevada experience extreme cases of this. There, the natural condition of the desert, which is to cool considerably at night, is changing. As a result of so much heat released into the air from the ground after the sun sets, these cities no longer experience nighttime desert cooling. So humans must use more energy to control indoor temperatures while the animals that have evolved in this climate find survival more difficult.

Helpful Notes: Outside the Southwest

How does cement affect the environment you live in?

In more temperate climates, large amounts of cement limit the amount of storm water absorption into the ground and can contribute to flooding. Cement lots create a steamy and lifeless environment.

Photographs 1.10 Before, a hot, gravel-mulched landscape. Courtesy of Charles Gallagher and Gina Ortiz

Photographs 1.11 After, a cool organic-mulched landscape. Courtesy of Charles Gallagher and Gina Ortiz

As we transition into sustainable communities, we must reduce the amount of concrete around our homes, perhaps recycling the busted-up concrete, called urbanite, for pathways in our gardens. We need more gardens and less cement to live sustainably. Our gardens need big rocks to separate the pathways from the gardens. We can break up the cement that currently frames our homes and buildings, and exists in vast unused parking lots, and use those pieces to form garden beds and inviting pathways. By replacing cement driveways with gravel, cement sidewalks with crusher fine or mulch, rock mulch with organic mulch, and cement patios with crusher fine, brick, or flagstone, we increase visual interest, allow more storm water absorption into the soil, and cool surrounding temperatures. (Note: Mulch can be anything that covers the ground – gravel, glass, woodchips. When we refer to mulch in this book, we generally mean organic mulches – woodchips, straw, pecan shells – that can break down to make soil. But that is not the only benefit of mulch. We discuss the importance of mulches more thoroughly in Chapter Three.)

Our Home Farms
From Melanie

To make the installation of Melanie's design more affordable, and to practice sustainability, we decided to use urbanite to line the paths. Zoe spoke with a representative of the City of Albuquerque, who said we could take some concrete that had just been removed from a sidewalk. So we drove to a construction location, busted up chunks of the concrete with a sledgehammer, loaded it in Zoe and Bard's truck, and unloaded it in Melanie's backyard. In about an hour and a half, Zoe and Melanie together moved about a ton of concrete, which was a very good workout! It was free and made beautiful bordered pathways.

Here is another aspect of the Earth element considerations on Melanie's property. Melanie's garage has been converted into a studio apartment for guests. A paved driveway leads right up to the western entrance of this casita.

Photograph 1.12 Busted-up Concrete, Called Urbanite, Being Installed in Melanie's Backyard during Design Implementation

In the summer, the sun bakes the concrete all day long, heating up the air all around the casita. In the afternoon, the hottest sun of the day blasts through the poorly insulated window as well as bouncing heat and reflective light up from the cement into the adjacent house. To keep this space comfortable for living, Melanie must invest a lot of money in cooling.

One option is to remove the concrete driveway, the source of this heat reflection. However, this approach felt too expensive and difficult to Melanie at this time.

To lessen the impact of the western heating in the summer, Melanie decided to build a shade structure to the west of the casita that would also shade the kitchen window in the house from the southern sun. She worked with a contractor to design this structure such that the shade cloth could be removed in the winter, allowing the southern sun to warm the casita and the house in the winter, and allowing views of the sky and neighboring trees at this time of year. During the hottest part of the summer, when the sun's rays in the afternoon reach the farthest, Melanie uses bamboo shades rolled down along the sides of the shade structure to protect the casita still more from the heat reflected off the driveway. This also creates a private outdoor living space for guests in the casita. Homedepot.com is a good source for inexpensive shade cloth and patio blinds.

Photograph 1.13 The Shade Structure Outside Melanie's Casita

A concrete patio in Melanie's backyard serves as the transition zone from the house to the garden. Although it makes a good surface for a patio table, it is very hot in the summer, so she is considering removing the concrete and replacing it with a wood porch or leaving this area as dirt. In the meantime, she has installed a shade sail to protect and cool this area.

Another important building element is the shed, where she stores gardening supplies. We also needed to make sure the garden design would work well with the pathway that goes around the house to the driveway, where supplies are brought into the backyard.

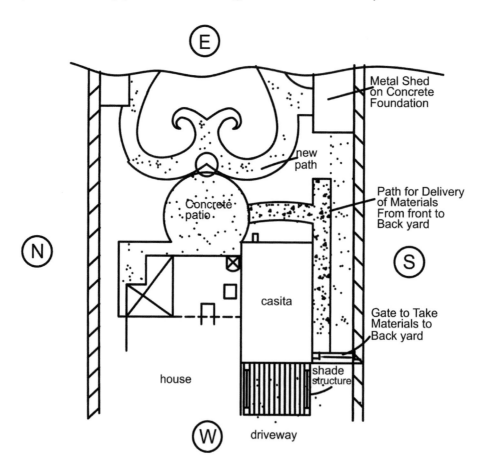

Drawing 1.10 The Area Around Melanie's Casita

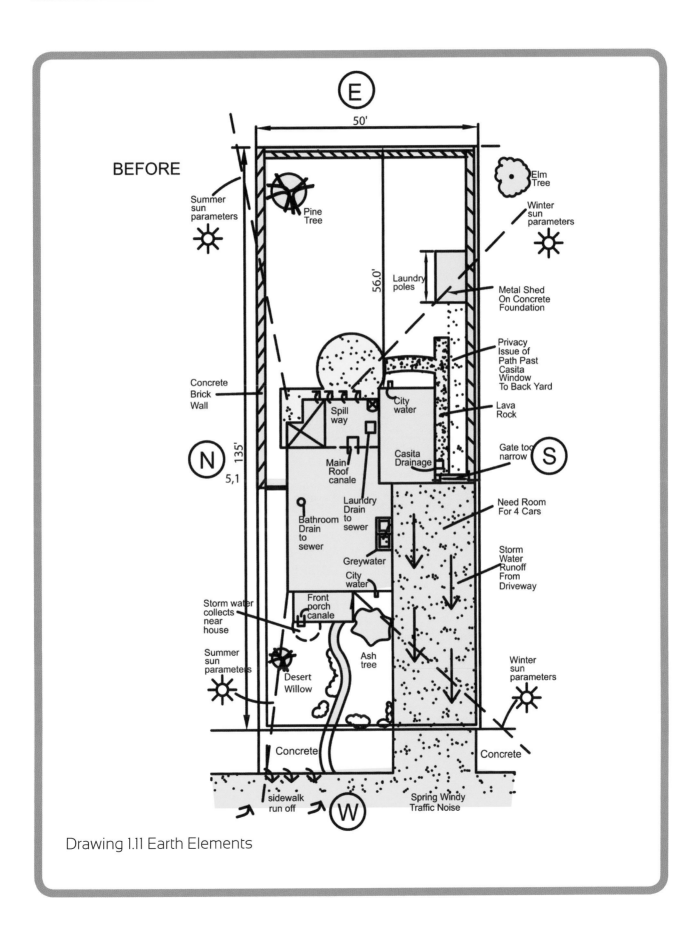

Drawing 1.11 Earth Elements

Soil

We can't farm effectively without examining the soil, and the site assessment phase is the time to consider your soil. To get to know your soil, you can measure it for three things: structure, pH, and nutrition. Of the three measurements, structure is the only one I would insist on. The other two depend on your personal interest.

The percentage of clay, sand, or loam in your soil is what determines the *soil structure*. Knowing your soil structure will tell you about any issues you might have with drainage, and what plants will and won't thrive on your property.

You can do a test of your soil structure with zero dollars and about 15 minutes. Take a sample of soil from where you plan to put your garden bed. Place it in a glass jar. Fill it with water and cover it with the lid. Shake it a bit and then let it sit for 15 minutes. Sand and rocks fall out first and make a bottom layer. The next level is loam. Above that, the clay layer sits. Organic matter floats. Ideally, you have equal parts of all these materials. If you're like most people who don't have that mix, Chapter Seven discusses soil-building methods.

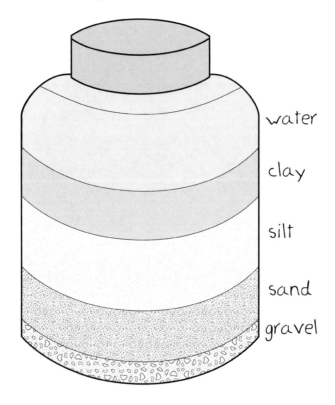

Drawing 1.12 Soil Jar Test.

You can measure the pH balance of your soil to determine the acidity or alkalinity of your soil with a home kit purchased on-line or from a garden store, or contact your local County Extension Office to have an agent test it for you. The pH scale ranges from 0 to 14, with 7 being perfectly neutral. Lower numbers indicate more acidity in the soil and higher numbers indicate more alkalinity in the soil. Most plants do best in soil which is slightly acidic, within the range of pH 6.3 – 6.8. Dry climates tend towards alkaline soil while wet climates tend towards acidic soil. Pine trees create acidic soil.

For a small additional fee, an extension agent can list any harmful chemicals found in your soil. You can also observe what grows on your property. If you only have pioneer species, the first species to grow on land thoof has been disturbed or stripped of top soil which tend to thrive on nutrient-poor soil, you will know that your soil does not have the resources it needs to grow nutrient-rich food. You can also detect low nutrient levels in veggie gardens when leaves turn yellow as they grow. Most desert soils have low nutrient value because there is little organic matter in the soil. Land that has already been farmed may lack nutrients because they have been used up. Flood plains tend to contain too much clay. Whatever the issue, too sandy, too much clay, not enough nutrients, the answer, as you will see in Chapter Eight, is always to add more organic matter. Without organic matter, microorganisms have nothing to eat or break down to release and create soil nutrients. With added organic matter, like compost or mulch, microorganisms have all they need to do their work of making nutrient-rich soil.

Summary of the Earth Element

With the Earth element 'Earth', you will look at existing structures that will become destination points for your pathways. You will learn about the trees on your property and neighboring properties and evaluate their value. You will plan how to care for the trees you will keep and sometimes eliminate those that are bringing more negative than positive attributes to the property. You will assess the distribution and quantity of cement on the site and see how to eliminate as much of it as possible, and lessen the negative impacts of the concrete you decide to keep. Finally, you will look at the soil on your property and get a clear picture of what you have to work with. All these investigations will help you place farm elements and develop your land for food production.

Intersection of the Elements: Looking for Microclimates

As you identify how each of the four Earth elements affects your property, you will notice microclimates in your space. For example, you may have a relatively moist and cool area in one location, a shaded but dry area in another, a hot and dry area somewhere else, and so forth. Later, you will start placing farm elements in the landscape to take advantage of these microclimates or to deliberately change or develop microclimates.

 **Our Home Farms**
From Melanie

For example, in Melanie's backyard the coolest zone was under the Ponderosa pine tree. We decided this would be the best place to locate the bees and, as previously mentioned, half of the chicken coop.

Exercise 1.4 Evaluating the Earth Element on Your Property

1. On your site plan, make sure each of these items is identified:

   - Existing structures

   - Trees

   - Cement pathways, driveways, patios, and other surfaces

2. Sketch the "paths of least resistance" where formal pathways do not exist.

3. Identify any "heat islands" and consider what changes you might want to make to these areas.

4. Identify any trees you may wish to remove, or shaded areas around trees where you will want to locate seating areas but not garden beds.

5. Think about the implications of the locations of these features, and how you will use or interact with them, for how you may want to locate your garden beds and other elements in your home farm design.

6. Think back through each of the four Earth elements, Water, Fire, Air and Earth, and jot down any additional notes about how they impact your space.

7. Then identify any microclimates on your site plan.

Chapter Two: Design Step Two

What to Include in the Design

Overview

In Step One of the design, you observed the land in detail and asked, "What exists already?" In Step Two, you will look at what you are about to add to your site. This process is about assessing your needs as a resident, choosing which farm elements you wish to include in your home farm, and determining the resources you will need to accomplish this, as well as ideas on how to acquire those resources cost-effectively.

Assess Your Needs as a Resident

 **Overview**

First, assess your personal needs. Before you think about chickens or vegetables, think about including yourself in your landscape and the impact you will have on your site. Farmers do not farm from within their homes or their offices. They are successful at getting the most out of their environment because they are outside, being part of the environment. You and the other residents of your home are the first element in your new farm. You are wildlife – an element of nature. Consider your particular physical, lifestyle, and spiritual needs, as well as the needs of your family members, housemates, and pets. Sometimes, these types of needs are called "invisible structures." How will your design meet the needs of these invisible structures?

Metaphor for the Space

Often, it is helpful to identify a metaphor that describes what you want this space to do for you. Are you looking for a sanctuary to get away from the stresses of life, and to sit, work, or eat quietly? Maybe you want your garden to be a gathering place that will serve as a setting for social get-togethers. If so, what kind of social events will it accommodate: informal meals where family and friends visit while children play together? Or, sophisticated cocktail parties? Do you need a play space, an area for practicing tai chi, working out, or training your dog? It is likely you will want your outdoor space to serve a combination of functions. The important thing is that the space fits you, the resident. A successfully designed farm is used frequently. It feels like an extension of your home living space. If a designer creates a plan that is beautiful but not practical or useful for the people living there, it is not a good design. Your site will develop as you do, and you will continue to modify your design the more you live in it and with it.

 ## Special Physical Needs

Consider whether you or any of the residents in your home have any special physical needs. Are all of the residents able to walk and squat well? In most arid land gardens, I prefer to use depressed growing beds that catch water. However, raised beds, especially those bordered with insulating strawbales, allow a person to sit on the edge of the beds or reach into the garden from a chair. These can be an excellent solution where there are special physical needs. Wide, flat paths in a garden allow friends to walk side-by-side, and create access for walkers, wheelbarrows, and wheelchairs. Crusher fine (a type of very fine gravel), compacts very well and can be easily navigated by those on wheels. Bard recently installed a design for a blind client. Paths were wide and he made sure that the steps between the patio and the path were even. He planted specifically to attract as many birds as possible because the homeowner enjoys identifying birds by their songs.

Photograph 2.1 Raised Beds Can Accommodate Gardeners with Special Needs - Courtesy of Bob Morgan

 **Children**

If children live in or visit the home regularly, they need their own area. Home farms create an enormously interesting environment to explore and experience, but most children also need a space to run around and roll on the ground. Fields, big or small, welcome this romping activity. We have a mulch "field" at Mother Nature Gardens in the middle of our garden beds that welcomes 25 chairs for farming classes or a half a dozen children playing soccer. It is cool, takes lots of traffic, and is completely maintenance free. With a higher investment of water and upkeep, you can have the cooling comfort of a green lawn. To keep green grass with the least amount of supplemental water, use native grasses. A mix of buffalo grass, a low growing, clay-loving grass that spreads by runners, and blue grama, a bunching, sand-loving grass that spreads by seed, assures the most coverage in the widest area. The species most in alignment with the environment will, in time, dominate the area. Maintain a grass patch as one section of a living quilt of garden beds and grasses. Try to grow your native grass patch in a large, depressed basin that gathers water during rains or greywater deposits. The amount of water you need to maintain a green lawn will differ depending on how much traffic it receives and how short you cut the grass. The shorter the grass, the more water it takes to maintain. So allow for a more wild-looking yard where the grass is allowed to go to seed. The lowest, water-use, native lawn will still require a thorough wetting once a week from late May through August. Native grasses take very little supplemental water after becoming established. These sustainable and water-conscious lawns create important places to play and rest. Playhouses can also add a great deal of interest to a backyard, and to a child's world.

Photograph 2.2 Children's Playhouse at Mother Nature Gardens

 Pets

Pets have their own needs as well. Dogs and cats sometimes require good garden fences to keep them out of growing areas. Alternately, you can make a sheltered pen where dogs can run and go to the bathroom when the owner isn't outside with them. Pets love grass almost as much as children, so a grass patch may be important for your pooch. Finally, all pets poop. If you have a dog, design a spot for his or her poop – then train your dog to poop there! This is the one time I suggest a gravel patch in yards because gravel makes it easier to scoop up after a dog.

Spiritual Aspects of the Space

In addition to the practical use of a site, it is also helpful and satisfying for many people to connect spiritually with the space. Throughout the design process of creating a garden sheltered from the sounds of the city and harsh elements, bordered and filled with green, you can create a sanctuary that facilitates your connection with a higher spiritual vibration that's so available in nature. If that doesn't interest you, skip over this section. But if connecting spiritually with your farm does interest you, let's take it a step further. What spiritual systems and traditions resonate with you, and what symbols do they use? Incorporate these symbols into the design as a visual reminder of the spirit element. Maybe there is a dull corner that you would like to energize with an altar dedicated to the deity or religion of your choice. My personal experience is that a garden will respond to and resonate with whichever spirits or saints you choose to honor there.

Photograph 2.3 Steve and Mary Dorch's beautiful "Zen Garden"

 ## Summary

After you study what is on your site, you will evaluate what will go onto the site. The most important consideration related to what belongs on the site is the needs of the residents. So, in this section, we looked at your needs for the use of the space, including physical, lifestyle, and spiritual needs. We discussed the importance of accommodating people with special physical needs, children, and pets. Make sure the design will work well for all of the creatures who live on your property.

Our Home Farms
From Melanie

In my home farm, several main factors created the orientation of the design:

1. I wanted the garden to have a focal point of a meditation space and altar, and for this to be located, on axis, with the line of sight from the back sunroom and back patio.

2. The symbol of the heart is very important to me.

3. I wanted this garden to be a place that would invite many visitors and help to foster community.

4. I wanted the center of the garden to be a Star of David planted with low-growing medicinal herbs.

5. I wanted the garden to accommodate holding workshops with at least 25 people, as well as to maintain an entertainment space for hosting dinners outside in the summer.

Drawing on these symbolic and practical elements, Zoe created a design of two large, intersecting hearts, with a meditation altar at one end and a Star of David in the center.

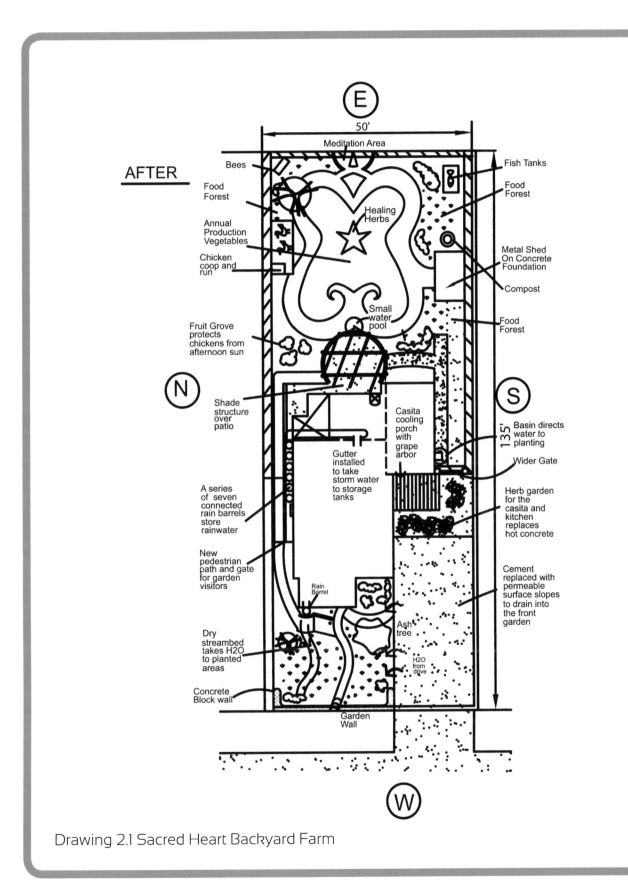

Drawing 2.1 Sacred Heart Backyard Farm

Exercise 2.1

1. Is there a particular metaphor that speaks to you about what you want your home farm to be and do in your life?

2. What specific activities or functions do you want your home farm to serve?

3. Will you have children in your home farm?

4. Will people with special medical or physical needs participate in your home farm?

5. Will you have pets in your home farm?

6. Will your home farm be designed to honor any spiritual beliefs or traditions?

Assessing the Home Farm Elements

 Overview

Next, list all the farm elements you hope to have. This will be an iterative process, since you will better understand what farm elements you may want to include as you learn more about the different farm elements later in this book. So, we recommend you mark this list to come back to once you have read the entire book. We will go over each of these elements briefly below, and the following chapters will describe them in detail:

- Outdoor living spaces, including play areas for children, recreation areas, eating areas, sacred space or meditation areas, and areas for entertaining.

- Water systems, including passive rainwater systems which use water as it runs off your home and structures; active rainwater harvesting systems, which capture, store, and direct water for future use; drip systems, which use either rainwater, well water, or city water to channel water through hoses and piping to irrigate specific locations; and greywater systems, which recycle water already used for one purpose to be used again for another purpose.

- Food forests, where you can grow fruits, nuts, and vegetables in the same location by layering plants of different heights above and below ground.

- Annual vegetable production.

- Chickens; and

- Honeybees that produce honey and other bee products.

Outdoor Living Spaces

In assessing your personal needs, we affirmed that you are a significant element of your patch of green. So there needs to be a spot for you in that space – a place to work out of the sun, the rain, and maybe even the cold, and a place not to work at all, but just to enjoy being outside. Having outdoor living spaces helps you get outside and observe and interact with your garden so you can make adaptations to grow food more successfully. Furthermore, your outdoor living spaces on the east and west sides of your house can double as shade structures that buffer your home from the sun to cool it during the summer.

Water systems

A farm is only as productive as its watering system. We discuss passive methods of harvesting rainwater in Chapter Three as part of the design process. Chapter Four, outdoor livings spaces, includes tips for simple greywater systems. Chapter Five looks at how to capture and redistribute rainwater. Chapter Six outlines do-it-yourself irrigation systems.

 Food Forest

"Food forest" is a term used to describe edible landscaping, which provides a "wild" food production area of your home farm. Plants and shrubs in a food forest are perennials so they use less water and nutrients than annual vegetables. In fact, they require very little input or effort after installation. Yet, they are selected to yield fruits, veggies, and medicinal plants throughout the growing season. Amazingly, in a food forest, it is possible to grow food in seven layers in one small area, working from the upper canopy down into the ground. In Chapter Seven we will provide very specific examples of how this works and the types of plants that can be included in a food forest.

This well-established, intelligent system maximizes food production in small spaces by growing food vertically. You layer your space and pack in your production. This wall of green functions to block unwanted views, shade hot walls, deflect aggressive winds, and muffle noise, making even a small food forest amazingly useful. Food forests become more valuable with time and thus are an important asset to pass down to the next generation. In some parts of the world, there are multi-generational food forests.

 Annual Vegetable Production

When you consider annual vegetable production, think of diverse, thriving communities of plants in beds instead of rows of a single species. Plants are like people. They function best in diverse communities where their strengths complement each other and their weaknesses can be balanced. Mixing flowers, vegetables, and herbs all together makes your vegetable production more resistant to pests and disease and your soil healthier. We use a system of vegetable gardening that does not follow a paradigm of straight rows and precision, but has a more wild feel, like nature. Design beds so that you can reach all plants from pathways, without stepping on the dirt and compressing the soil.

Chicken Production

The next thing to consider is chicken production. Chickens not only can give you eggs and meat, they quickly and effectively decompose green waste. They close the loop of production and regeneration on your farm. Chickens thrive on kitchen scraps and green waste from the garden. In return, they produce delicious, protein-rich eggs and nitrogen-rich manure for growing more food. It is a win/win trade, which doesn't even take into account the entertainment factor of their habits and behaviors. They are really fun to watch! See Chapter Ten for detailed information about raising chickens in even a tiny space.

Raising Honey Bees

If you think you need a huge space to tend honeybees, think again. Small production beekeeping has gone on since the time of ancient Egypt. Experts link recent and dramatic die-offs of honeybees, often called "hive collapse," to many theories. One includes the mistreatment of bees for accelerated production by commercial honey farmers. Backyard beekeeping is one answer to this threat, just as home farming is one of the answers to the dangers of many forms of large-scale commercial food production.

Bees can provide honey for you as well as wax for skin products and candles. They also produce pollen, an excellent source of protein, and propolis, which is a natural and local source of antibiotics and antifungal remedies. We can also thank bees for pollinating a third of our food production. If raised properly, bees pose little threat to homeowners and neighbors. A detailed introduction to beekeeping is provided in Chapter Eleven.

Drawings 2.2, 2.3, 2.4, and 2.5 How a Landscape Develops in Layers

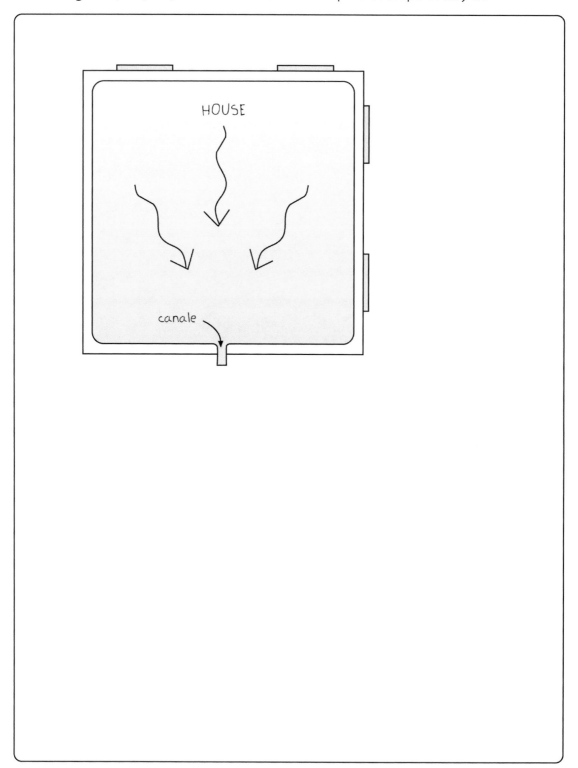

2.2 Original Landscape

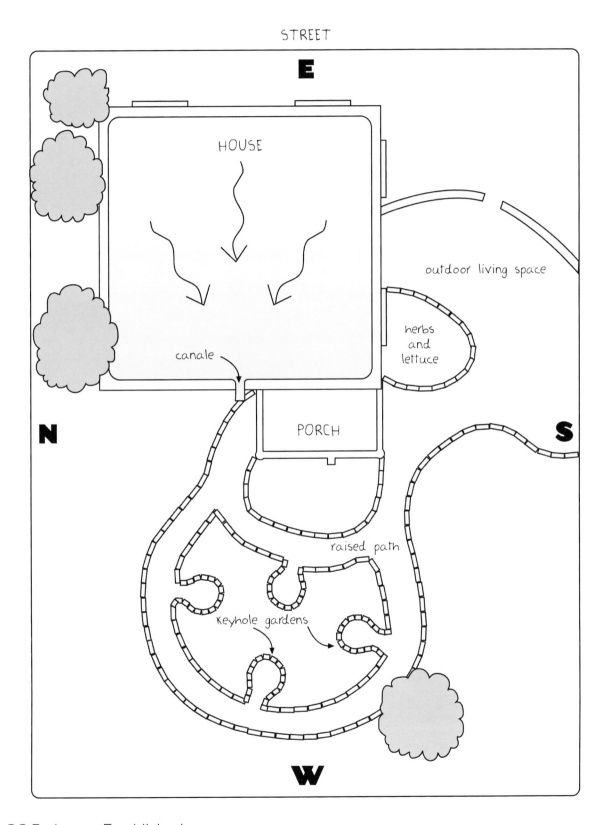

STREET

E

HOUSE

outdoor living space

herbs
and
lettuce

canale

N

PORCH

S

raised path

Keyhole gardens

W

2.3 Pathways Established

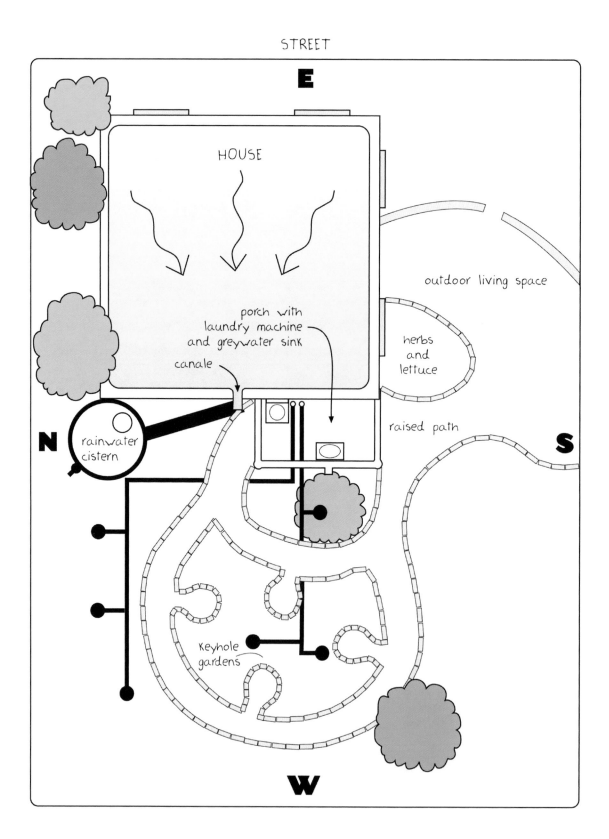

STREET

E

HOUSE

porch with
laundry machine
and greywater sink

canale

N

rainwater
cistern

outdoor living space

herbs
and
lettuce

raised path

S

Keyhole
gardens

W

2.4 Water Distribution Systems Installed

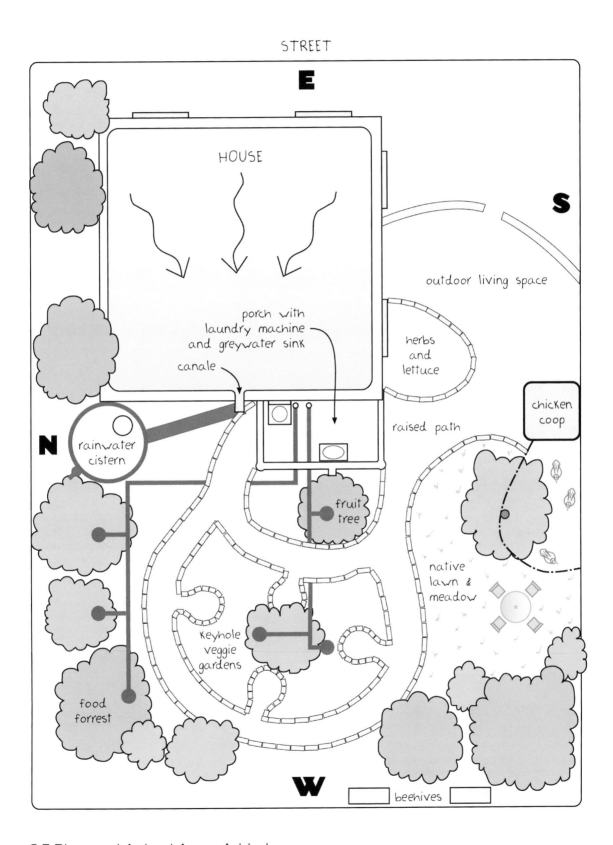

STREET

E

HOUSE

S

outdoor living space

porch with
laundry machine
and greywater sink

herbs
and
lettuce

canale

chicken
coop

rainwater
cistern

N

raised path

fruit
tree

native
lawn &
meadow

Keyhole
veggie
gardens

food
forrest

W

beehives

2.5 Plant and Animal Areas Added

Our Home Farms
From Melanie

In my home farm I decided I wanted to include all of these elements in some way, shape, or form, although I didn't anticipate I would implement them all fully during the first season. In the first season, I put in a shade structure for an outdoor living space, a chicken coop, a meditation altar, and some elements of a food forest. In the second season, I added honeybees, a medicinal herb garden for the bees, and additional medicinal plants and herbs in my food forest.

 Exercise 2.2

Make a list of the elements you want to include in your home farm, both in the short and long term. In the next chapter, you will learn how to place these things, even if they won't be implemented for several years in your design.

Identifying the Resources You Will Need

As you read through this book, you will get a sense of what resources you will need to implement each aspect of your design, including soil, materials, lumber, irrigation supplies, etc.

To decide how you want to sequence the implementation of your design, it is helpful to itemize the resources you will need to accomplish each project you want to do. Keeping an ongoing list of these supplies will help you estimate and plan costs and labor. In keeping with our desire to encourage sustainability, we hope you don't go out and buy everything on your list at the nearest big box store. Share your list of materials needed with the people you know as well as local gardening clubs, farms, online forums, and other networking avenues to see how much you can collect, trade, share, convert, or buy secondhand. Most people attempting some level of sustainability have a storage spot in their yard for stockpiled materials. Becoming sustainable requires you to learn how to use and reuse what you already have, and acquire and trade for what you don't have.

 Rock

As a contracted landscaper, one thing we need in almost every design we install is rock in the form of 6- to 12-inch boulders. We use rock as borders for clearly defined pathways and waterways, and to create terraces on sloped land. Rock is the skeleton of almost every design we create and will likely be the skeleton of your design too.

Some folks are lucky enough to have rock on their land. Most towns have businesses that sell landscape rock. Our favorite rock source, as we've mentioned already, is urbanite, which is busted-up pieces of concrete gathered from construction sites or any place that concrete is no longer needed. It is free and a great way to recycle.

 Tools

Finally, what tools will you need to get the work done? Fortunately, tools can remain basic at first, since you can get a home farm started with a shovel, a rake, and a wheelbarrow. Trucks are extraordinarily valuable for hauling materials when creating a home farm. If you don't have a truck, sharing and trading are ways to keep initial expenses low while fostering community-based cooperation.

 Mulch & Compost

A farm needs good soil. Mulch insulates soil from heat, protects it from wind and rain erosion, and provides organic matter for micro-organisms to break down into better soil. No farm should be without it. Our area is blessed with a brilliant company, Soilutions (soilutions.net), that takes in green waste, which would otherwise end up in the city dump, and turns it into beautiful mulches and rich compost. Look for a company like this in your area. Counties and tree trimmers also grind tree trimmings and will usually give their product away for free. If you and some neighbors have a great deal of wood waste, you can rent a chopper for the day. There are many options for finding mulch before resorting to buying it by the bag.

You can begin to create your own compost in your first year of farming, and we will discuss how in Chapter Eight, Preparing the Veggie Garden. If you need fertile additions to your gardens before your mature compost is ready, look for horse farms that welcome people who haul away their manure. Be careful of cow manure and other commercial farm manures. They are often loaded with salts from animal salt licks, as well as unknown pharmaceuticals. Call your local nursery or extension agent to get advice about ethical compost sources.

Assessing the Resources You Have

To convert your yard to a home farm, you will invest significant resources into your land. Being upfront about what resources you have, and comparing those with what you need, helps ground the dream so you can create a time line and action plan to meet your goals. Identifying what you don't have is the first step in finding ways to manifest what you need creatively.

Unless you become an excellent free-cycler, organizer, and trader, your garden will require money. Money spent on the garden seems to be a trade-off with time and labor. If you have a well-paying career, you can hire a professional to design and install the landscape for you, and get results quickly. Hopefully, you'll find one who is knowledgeable about sustainable landscape practices and who will work with your vision and needs. The professional will buy all the materials where they can get a good product for a good price. Yet, if you want to do it on a shoe-string, it's possible to like Bard and I did. You are probably going to dedicate a lot of time and labor to the process. We hunted down and scavenged materials that sometimes sat in our yard a long time before they were put to use. You have to find the balance for your personal situation.

Exercise 2.3

List your:

- Available materials
- Available funds
- Available time
- Available labor
- Available tools
- Community resources for sharing information, labor, support, etc.

Sustainable Living by Habit

As you discuss and gather lists of all the materials you will need for your home farm implementation, think about what's already on hand, what is nearby, and opportunities to recycle. Not only does using recycled and available materials save money, the closer the source of your materials, the less embodied energy they represent and, therefore, the more sustainable they are. You can visit a dozen different subsistence villages throughout the world and you will see a dozen different types of homes because the local people use the materials they have access to around them. Learn to use the materials around you and to turn the problem into the solution.

Sustainable living takes time. When you give up some of your high embodied-energy conveniences, there is an exchange of how you spend your time. Sustainable living is slower, more grounded, and connected. Between watering, doing laundry outdoors, and seasonal garden maintenance, Bard and I spend about 8 to 10 hours a week farming. Most new systems require learning new habits, so it's often a matter of redirecting your energy.

Many people are looking for work following the recent epic collapse in our economy. I have watched the emotional toll these economic challenges take on skillful and intelligent friends who want to work, look for work with great discipline, and can't find it. Growing healthy food is not only a therapeutic stress reliever, it is work that is desperately needed to improve the health of our community, and is an excellent way to supplement a shrinking grocery budget. Growing food can be done part-time, while you are a primary care giver for your child or starting a small business from home.

 ## Slow Living Farms

Recently Bard and I spent the winter working on a farm in west-central Mexico while our work in the states slowed to a trickle. We stayed, and considered "home" for that time, at a homestead called Slow Living Farms. There, 10 acres of citrus and mango trees, vines of passion fruit, and dozens of local production fruit trees covered the mountain slope that looked out over the Pacific Ocean. At Slow Living Farms, Wally Carlson and Amaranth Rose learned to sustain themselves out of necessity. There was no big box hardware or auto parts store, no large-scale grocery store, no fully stocked drugstore nearby to meet their needs. They live by adaptation and the belief that everything they needed was right there on their property. They stockpiled old tools, materials, and electronics and went to these broken-down units for parts when repairs were needed. Parts for cars became plumbing parts and parts for electronics became parts for cars.

After experiencing their lifestyle and coming back to our fully commercialized city, we began to notice how often we immediately and unquestioningly go out to buy something when we have a need. We began to pause between needing and buying to include an intermittent step where we asked ourselves, "What do we have right here, right now that would work for what we need?" On Slow Living Farms, sometimes they wait a while for the right part or the right ingredient to manifest itself, but waiting is the only option. It is more of a conscious effort for us to wait for our needed part in our US city because the option to consume is so immediate. However, we are now sold on this belief and so we resist immediate consumption in favor of letting the things we need come to us. And they do. Of course we still shop, but we've adapted our lifestyle to allow for more sustainability.

 ## Sharing Labor, Tools, and Information

People who are building home farms can share resources as well as labor. At the writing of this book, a group of friends are setting up a work/trade arrangement where every couple of weeks the group will go to one member's house to work, sharing labor like the Amish. The success of this type of idea lies in the proximity of the members. The closer you are to another person, the easier it is to live in community with them.

Tools are a great resource to share. For example, find a group of people in your neighborhood who want to tear up some cement around their homes, pitch the idea to them, and then one day, go out together and rent a jack hammer and move from one house to the next breaking up concrete. You might want to pay for a communal truck. Begin to look at your community as a resource. And remember all the information available in your library.

If you are doing something great at your home, host an open house. Many, many people who have visited our home during open houses have expressed great gratitude for being able to see our work and get inspired to start their own work. Every neighborhood could benefit from home farmers opening their doors from time to time to inspire others in their local community.

Our Home Farms
From Melanie

I began my home farm design with very few tools or resources, both in terms of time and money, while working full-time during the day. I borrowed a wheelbarrow from a neighbor down the street. Zoe located a source of broken concrete and we hauled two truckloads to my place in Zoe and Bard's truck. A local soil supply company provided compost and mulch in trade for business services I offered. Cardboard was donated by Whole Foods and hauled in a truck borrowed from a friend. A local nursery donated plants, and a local seed company donated seeds. During the first workshop about design, workshop participants brought tools and shovels to use, and I borrowed additional wheelbarrows from a local community garden. Subsequently a home farm friend donated several rain barrels, and another friend installed a basic rainwater harvesting system. Later in the summer, with a shortage of time before the chicken workshop was scheduled to run, and a recent donation of money from an interested party, I decided to invest in new materials for the chicken coop. Given more time, I would have preferred to use recycled and salvaged materials. I think this approach, of manifesting materials, resources, and support, is available to anyone who is really committed to creating their home farm.

Chapter Three:

Creating the Design

Overview

After all the observing, assessing, and list making that you completed in the previous chapters, you are now ready to learn the techniques and tools to put your plans into a design! Remember, the quality of your design will depend on the thoroughness of your initial observation, and your ongoing practice of observing and responding to the unique opportunities and characteristics of your site. The best design begins in your gut in direct response to your observation, rather than in your head, is clarified on paper, and only then is implemented in physical space (when our bodies take action). As you go through this chapter, you will start to see the big picture of your design: dream it, map it, and organize its creation into a practical sequence of action steps. If parts of the design are cloudy in the beginning, that's okay. Trust that as you continue with the process, clarity will come. All designs change somewhat as they're implemented because during implementation you learn things about your land, desires, and resources that you didn't anticipate in the dreaming stage. Yet, every adventure needs a starting point and a vision. The design is the vision on paper.

In this chapter, we'll look at passive rainwater harvesting techniques that will help you use rainwater as efficiently as possible and lower soil erosion, including some basic earthworks appropriate for small and medium-sized properties. Know that watering considerations can and should help shape your design. Then, you will experiment with placing the different farm elements according to where they will best thrive, as well as suit your individual needs. Finally, you will connect these farm elements with beautiful and functional pathways. Once the design is complete, you will create an action plan, step-by-tiny-step, and a timeline to divide your grand scale project into manageable chunks of work and expense.

Passive Rainwater Harvesting

In the Southwest, to maximize life in a certain area of your home farm, you must first design for that area to hold the greatest amount of water possible. **Passive rainwater harvesting** uses land shaping, or **earthworks,** to slow and control storm water, and direct it into the ground instead of into the street drain. Well-designed passive rainwater harvesting rarely holds water on the surface for long. Water is directed to densely planted, thickly-mulched basins that act as sponges to absorb moisture quickly. The earth then stores the water like a savings bank that plants draw from in times of drought. This approach to managing water also promotes recharging of our shallow aquifers. Once water is in the ground, it can no longer erode the soil and fill waterways with sediment. Furthermore, healthy soils filter out the pollutants that drain off of roads and parking lots so waterways stay cleaner. By harvesting rainwater passively, you make something valuable (free, clean water) out of something that can be destructive (uncontrolled storm waters).

During your site assessment, you noticed what storm water currently does when it falls on your property unmanaged. Next you will take the reins (i.e. your shovel) and start making the water go exactly where you want it to go. The earthworks you choose to incorporate will affect, if not shape, your design. Every property requires its own unique set of earthworks.

 ## Protect Structural Foundations

As you move earth around on your site, protect your home first. Due to undirected storm water, soil often erodes around the foundation, which can allow rainwater to pool against the foundation, compromising its structural integrity over time. If the soil has eroded around your foundation, use any poor soil from excavated garden beds or other areas on your property to build up the elevation against your home. Make sure the ground level is high enough within a four-foot-wide perimeter around your home to keep water away from your foundation. If you have a stucco home, do not build the soil up so high, however, that you have soil against the stucco. Moisture in the dirt can ruin a stucco job.

If you create growing beds next to your home, construct them so they slope away from the house toward the outside of each bed such that the deepest area of the bed sits farthest away from the house wall, beyond the four-foot perimeter around your home where you are directing water away from the foundation.

Photograph 3.1 An Against-the-House Growing Bed

 Surge Basins

Surge basins collect large volumes of water draining from canale or downspouts that do not lead to a cistern. They also catch water that overflows from a rain barrel or cistern. They are designed to catch and slow high velocity water before it moves into the rest of the landscape. Because surge basins are simply a pooling point, they *always* include an overflow that leads to other earthworks.

To make a surge basin:

1. Start several feet away from the house wall. The water will reach this basin through a directing gutter or a brick- or rock-lined depression from the high land around the house to the low basin.

2. Dig a large, wide basin big enough to slow down the amount of water it will receive from the roof space above. Consider the size of the surrounding area in determining the size of the basin. A larger yard needs a bigger surge basin. In general, when planning surge basins, bigger is better, but a small yard only needs a small surge basin. Smaller basins that receive high velocity water may require small rock walls to hold the surge.

   As you dig, remember you will fill some of this depression back up with rock, so use your legs and abdominal muscles (not your back) and work that shovel!

3. Level the bottom of the basin so the entire basin will fill evenly.

4. Dig sponges in the bottom of basin. See the section on page 100 of this chapter that describes what a sponge is.

5. Use the soil you've removed to protect the house foundation and create berms elsewhere in the yard. See the section on page 97 of this chapter that describes how berms are created as part of the process of building swales.

6. Finally, create an overflow for water to move out of the basin. Do not make the overflow directly in line with where water enters the basin. This would create more of a river flow than a pooling basin. Instead, offset the overflow from the inlet. This will make the water turn before it exits the basin. Every time water turns, velocity slows, sediment drops out, and the water becomes oxygenated. Make the overflow at a height of half or two-thirds the depth

of the basin so that when water stops flowing in, some will remain pooled at the bottom of the basin. Use a line level and string to make sure the overflow is lower than the inlet. Plants placed along the edge of the basin, or even hearty shrubs planted inside the basin, will benefit from the water collection in the basin.

7. Fill the basin with mulch and no fabric. Mulch acts as a sponge, absorbs water, and builds soil.

Photograph 3.2 A Surge Basin and Dry Streambed

Dry Streambeds

Often, surge basins overflow into dry streambeds that act like arteries taking water directly to planting beds. If you pay attention to landscapes in the area, you will surely see decorative streambeds that don't hold water (some are even convex). To be decorative and practically effective, the streambeds you create must hold water, flow from a water source, and lead to a planted basin.

Here is how you can make a streambed that will serve to channel water into your garden:

1. Dig your streambed to be at least a couple of feet wide (the width depends on the volume of water moving through it – for more volume, make the streambed wider) and deep enough that it will still hold water after you lay fabric and rock in it.

2. Create a 2% slope toward the destination point. A 2% slope drops 2 inches for every 10 feet of distance. This is called rise over run. To make a 2% slope, you'll need a couple of long sticks, string, a marker, a line level, and a partner.

   a. Place the sticks side by side and with your marker, make a straight line across both sticks.

   b. Tie the string around the mark on the first stick. This is your "nose" stick and string. Cut the tail of the string to be approximately 10 feet long plus a few inches for holding on to.

   c. On the second stick, the tail stick, measure two inches above your initial mark and mark it with a second mark. Hold the tail end of the string against this higher mark.

   d. Set your first stick on the ground at the top of the streambed, and the second on the ground in the streambed at the length of the10-foot string.

   e. Put your line level on the string. It will read level when the second stick sits two inches lower than the first. Experiment with moving the string up and down while watching the effects on your line level to get a feel for how the line level works. If your line level is not reading level, you will have to dig down (most likely) or build soil up underneath the tail stick.

3. Now place your nose stick where your tail stick just was and your tail stick 10 more feet down stream. Continue this process until you reach the outlet of the streambed, where it deposits. If possible, build your streambed so it turns back and forth along the way, before it reaches its destination. This will give you the benefits of turning water, described earlier, as well as visual appeal.

4. Put sponges (see the description on page 100 of this chapter), where you want to slow the water down.

5. Seed along the edge of the streambed with hardy, local wildflowers for future blossoms.

6. Streambeds can be filled with stone or just mulch. Include no fabric where you want the water to infiltrate.

Depressed Planting Basins

In the dry areas of this country, depressed growing beds work best because they capture and keep water better than raised beds. Back east, in the Midwest, or in the South, gardeners benefit from raised beds that can help prevent plants from drowning and stop soil from leaching away needed nutrients due to dozens of inches of yearly rainfall. Raised beds are generally a bad habit to bring into arid climates, although they are important for gardeners in any region who, because of physical limitations, cannot comfortably bend down to work in depressed beds.

Even where raised beds are called for, line the raised beds with straw bales or insulated wooden paneling, but keep food forests depressed. Planting on mounds increases soil exposure to the sun, which then increases evaporation and soil temperature. Mounds also shed water immediately. If you are in an arid climate, it works best to shape land like a chalice that receives and holds water. The Hopi waffle gardens used this concept – their gardens literally looked like waffles, with many small, squared-off growing areas that held water. Don't forget, any area that holds water must also include an outlet. If possible, create every outlet so the overflow will move into another planted basin. Connect your basins with curving dry streambeds like meandering, pooling rivers.

Photograph 3.3 Raised Pathway and Depressed Growing Beds

Raised Pathways

Sometimes the easiest way to make a basin is to raise a pathway. Keep your pathways high and dry around your depressed planting basins. Although finishing your pathways will come last, you will begin to build them up as you construct your garden beds and move earth around in your home farm. You can fill pathways with just about anything to raise them: gravel you remove from somewhere else, cardboard, old clothes, and waste paper. My pathways at home are full of old clothing, junk mail, and other refuse, which are all sources of carbon. Worms seek out carbon. So carbon-heavy pathways become a feeding center for worms, which then flourish in the garden beds and continuously produce new fertile soil. Border pathways with 6- to 12-inch boulders, pieces of urbanite, or whatever material you have on site that will appeal to the eye, depending on the garden size, while defining the elevation change between pathways and depressed beds. Fill the space between the rocks with low-quality dirt removed when digging a basin, cardboard, or torn clothing (my favorite). Later on, for a finished look, you can cover the paths with crusher fine, a colorful gravel that compresses well, or mulch. The garden beds defined by the paths will need to be amended with compost and mulch to make them ready for optimal growing and water retention.

 ## Rock Terraces

Sloped lands offer greater challenges for catching rainwater and holding soil. In traditional gardening and farming, Pueblo Indians of the desert Southwest make a single rock dam by laying a low line of stones across a slope *on contour*. The contour of the land is a line of equal elevation across the hillside. The line runs perpendicular to how a snow sled would speed down a hillside. You may have seen images of terraced mountainsides in Peru, Nepal or Vietnam that give a dramatic example of this method. The size of stone chosen depends on the steepness of the slope and the amount of water it needs to hold back. Sticks and soil washing down bare hillsides catch behind the rocks, forming small dams of fertile soil. The dams then catch water. With maintenance and seeding, these areas quickly become life belts across a slope.

Photograph 3.4 Terracing at Jennifer Coston's Home, Before

Photograph 3.5 Terracing at Jennifer Coston's Home, After

For a true terrace on sloped lots, exaggerate this ancient technique with tall boulders (4 to 12 inches tall) or stacked stone . Flatten out the land above the terrace by cutting into the high point of the slope and build up the low point against the rock terrace, laid on contour until the land is formed like wide steps instead of a hill. Stonewalls can terrace land in expressive curves that offer infinite visual interest, in addition to collecting water with great efficiency.

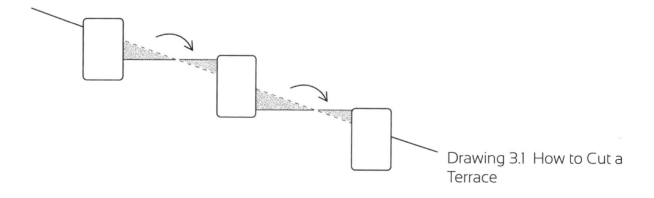

Drawing 3.1 How to Cut a Terrace

⊚ Swales

Swales are beneficial for sloped lands, to use instead of terracing or on large properties where they can be installed much more quickly and cost-effectively than terraces. Essentially, a swale is a ditch dug on contour (see the section "Rock Terraces" above for a description of contours), where the dirt from the ditch is deposited down slope, creating a paralleled ditch/mound that runs along the contour of the land. Swales can go for great distances and, with the help of machinery, they can be made fairly quickly.

To make a swale, begin by finding the desired contour line on the land. To do this, you will need the same tools needed for creating a dry streambed – two tall sticks, string, a line level, and a couple of friends (three people total is ideal, one on each stick, and one reading the line level) – but you will use the sticks slightly differently. In the dry streambed, you were creating a slope so you began by making marks of equal elevation across your sticks, and then made a second mark higher up on the stick to find or create a drop in elevation. You used your line level on the 10-foot string to make the uneven stick marks even (thus assuring that the ground wasn't even but sloped).

To find the contour to dig your swale, you only need the initial marks.

1. Stretch your 10-foot string across the land, in a way that looks to you like it is even. Keep your nose stick stationary and move the tail stick up and down the slope until the line looks level.

2. Once you find level, mark both your nose and tail stick with a landscape flag or just a rock.

3. Move your tail stick to where your nose stick was and your tail stick 10 feet further across the slope and do it again until you have an entire line of flags or rocks across the slope. You are now looking at a marked contour!

4. Then, dig a trench along the flagged line. Dump the soil below grade so as the ditch gets lower, and the land downgrade gets higher, this process will form a berm. Ditches are generally three feet wide and as deep as the gardener has stamina for. Again, the location and amount of water falling on your property will help you determine the most appropriate size for the ditch.

5. Thoroughly stomp the berm you have created to pack the soil tightly together, and make the berm more solid.

6. Cover both the ditch and the berm with mulch and seed the ditch with native seed mixes.

7. Plant shrubs midway between the depth of the ditch and the top of the berm. This way, the shrubs will have access to extra water but won't have water standing against their trunks. This is also a good place to plant a line of trees, or you can plant them on contour just below the top of the berm. These trees benefit from the water that seeps into the ground in the ditch. Water below ground also obeys gravity and moves downhill right to the trees' roots. On a large, sloped property, a crisscross of swales makes an ideal canvas for a thriving orchard.

Photograph 3.6 A Swale

The Importance of Mulch

Deserts are known for flash floods when storms finally hit. Because water molecules adhere to other water molecules as well as to organic material, water will run right over the top of the desert. In this way, dry desert soil repels the absorption of water such that the desert dries out again in a surprisingly short period of time. The runoff also collects surface dust and increases the weight of the water, which increases its potential destructiveness.

To counter this tendency and keep water from getting away, it is important to add mulch, which is a keystone element in a sustainable landscape. We will note its benefits in chapter after chapter of this book. From a rainwater harvesting perspective, every bit of land that isn't taken up by pathway, a surge basin, streambed, or overflow should be covered with a layer of mulch three to four inches thick *without* landscaping fabric. This is because landscaping fabric effectively kills the soil underneath it by limiting the seepage of moisture into the soil and cooking the soil, which kills the beneficial microorganisms in the soil. Three to four inches of mulch retards weed growth as well if not better than landscaping fabric without destroying the soil. Bare dirt is susceptible to compaction and erosion by wind and rain. In contrast, rainwater cannot possibly move as quickly across a mulched area. The fibers of each individual piece of mulch catch the rain and become moist quickly. Once the soil surface is wet, because water attracts water, more water can seep downward into the soil. Because there is no landscape fabric, the mulch at the soil surface breaks down, creating healthy, aerated topsoil high in organic matter.

The healthier the soil, the more readily it absorbs water. All this organic matter and lively soil that improves rain absorption also helps retain moisture in the soil. First, the layer of mulch acts like an insulation blanket, cooling the soil temperature and shading it from the searing desert sun, which can dry out exposed soil 40 feet below the surface. Mulch reduces evaporation dramatically. Then, the organic matter in the soil gives the water something to hold onto when the sun tries to pull it into the atmosphere, just like the last drops of water cling to the side of a drinking glass even when the drinker turns the glass upside down. When you attempt to capture 100% of the rain that falls on your property to store it in the soil so that your trees and plants can use it long term, organic mulch is an essential part of the equation.

⊚ Sponges

A sponge is a hole outside of the root zone of a tree or shrub that is filled with organic matter like kitchen scraps and junk mail. The organic matter breaks down and feeds the worms. The worms create humus, which holds more water.

Sponges help rainwater soak into the soil and subsoil and stay there. This counters the tendency of water to want to run off the soil or only absorb into the very top inches of soil. Instead, a sponge acts as a straw that draws water immediately down to the deep roots of plants and trees. You can incorporate sponges near any existing plants or trees that seem to be suffering; and installing a nearby sponge should become a habit when you are planting new trees. The only limit to how many sponges you can add is your energy and commitment. As long as you are not cutting into roots to make the hole for the sponge, the more you make, the happier the tree will be. You can also install sponges in basins to quicken infiltration for heavy loads of storm water.

Photograph 3.7 A Sponge

Photograph 3.8 A Series of Sponges Before Being Covered with Dirt

To make a sponge:

1. Dig a hole just beyond the reach of a newly planted tree's root ball, going down as deep as you have the energy for, but at least 18 to 24 inches below the surface. Locating the sponge just beyond an existing root ball will force the tree roots to expand outward. For an established tree, the span of the roots is typically at the drip line of the tree's canopy, and the sponge can be located just beyond this perimeter.

2. Water the hole and let the water soak in.

3. Then, fill the hole with high-carbon waste: junk mail, paper, old clothes, or mulch. If you use old phone books, make sure to lay them vertically so that water can soak in easily.

4. Water the materials in the hole, and cover them with a shovel full of dirt and mulch.

5. Leave the sponge area slightly depressed so water finds it quickly. You may want to flag the sponge to help you remember where you placed it. Micro-organisms will quickly eat at the carbon and, in a season, can turn your trash into gorgeous, spongy soil.

6. To water the tree from that point on, water the sponge.

Determining Where to Place Farm Elements

 ## Evaluating Farm Element Needs

Place your farm elements in the design according to where they will most likely thrive. To do this successfully, look at everything each farm element needs in order to function, and what each element produces. As you do this evaluation, connections between farm elements become obvious. Understanding these connections clearly will help you place objects so the work on your farm flows very harmoniously.

For example, what does a chicken need? Shelter, diverse and nutritious food, dust for "bathing," grit for digestion, clean water, protection from predators, shade, fresh air, and a way to keep warm in winter. Hens need to scratch and, for that good flock feeling, they need other chickens. In return for having their needs met, hens provide eggs, meat, feathers, carbon dioxide, shallow tilling, and fertile manure.

Now look at what your veggie beds need. Each vegetable bed needs water, fertilizer, insect control, and weeding. Each bed produces food, green waste, and oxygen. These two farm elements, veggie beds and chickens, benefit from being close to one another. The veggie bed benefits from the chicken manure, the fact that chickens eat insects that are harmful to the growth of the vegetables, and from chickens cleaning it up at the end of the season, after the harvest, when they are allowed into the garden. The chickens benefit when it is easy to throw garden waste and pesky bugs into the chicken run. The oxygen of the plants keeps chickens' lungs healthy. Veggies and chickens can enjoy strong symbiotic relationships that create a supportive and sustainable web of life at your home.

To get the most out of this symbiotic relationship, make these farm elements close neighbors. Relationships like these, as well as understanding the micro-climates we observe on our site, help us place all our farm elements.

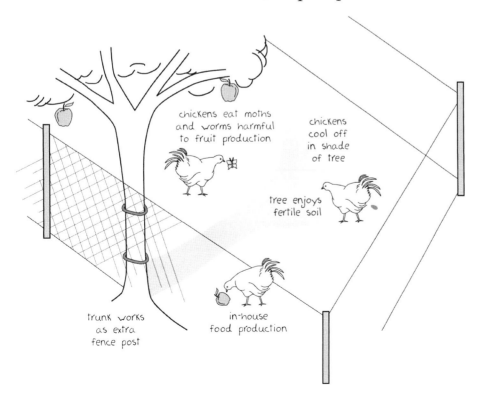

chickens eat moths and worms harmful to fruit production

chickens cool off in shade of tree

tree enjoys fertile soil

trunk works as extra fence post

in-house food production

Drawing 3.2
Chickens and Fruit Tree

Exercise 3.1

1. Use a separate sheet of paper for each farm element you plan to incorporate into your site and write that farm element at the top of the paper.

2. On the sheet designated for a particular farm element, list the needs and products of that element.

3. Then, notice how these needs and products overlap or intersect.

4. Experiment with optimal placement of your farm elements by moving the sheets of paper next to each other in different configurations and notice which placements have better relationships.

This exercise can help you see how your farm elements will work together, and indicate easy flows versus cumbersome or blocked flows.

 ## Success by Proximity

As you plan where to place your farm elements, remember that you will achieve *success by proximity.*

As a mother of an infant, I was constantly assessing and meeting my young son's needs as quickly as possible. We intuitively stuck very close to each other those first few years so I could achieve that. It is the same principle for other things we care for, although fortunately, nothing on the farm is quite as needy as a toddler. The greater a farm element's needs, the closer we must place it to us to facilitate its care and vitality. If I have veggie starts that need water twice a day, they will have a higher success rate if I have them right outside my back door and near a water source. Or imagine yourself rushing off to work in the morning. The chickens still need food and water but their coop sits in the furthest corner of your backyard. It is more likely you will forget to tend to them if they are out of sight and inconvenient to care for than if you pass them on the way to your car or bike. This is a busy world and most of us lead full, multi-tasking lives. Plan to make daily farming tasks as easy as possible by including convenience as a major factor in your design work.

As you sketch your design, imagine putting your arms around all the things that will need care on your farm. Draw them close in a big hug. Keep that cozy and close feeling as you start to place farm elements in the next section.

Stacking Functions

To help you get the most from your space, make sure that everything in your farm accomplishes more than one task. Everything is interconnected. So instead of asking a plant simply to give you food or a tree to give you shade, make each serve a minimum of three functions, or more if you can think of them. The plant now gives food, confuses pests from visiting a neighboring plant, and provides extra foliage that chickens love to eat. The tree casts shade, provides leaf matter to build rich soil, and blocks an unpleasant view. By consciously placing everything on your land to serve multiple functions, you will get much more accomplished with less input of time and energy. Although in cities and towns we farm in relatively small areas compared with our traditional idea of a farm, theoretically, there is no limit to the amount of life a space can hold, no matter its size. Stacking functions helps maximize growing capacity, fill niches, and make "waste" useful.

Forming Pathways

Imitating Patterns in Nature in the Pathways

In Chapter One, we identified destinations (house, garage, etc.) and located any existing pathways in the dirt. In this chapter, we began to place desired farm elements for future destinations. Now, let's look at connecting all of these elements with pathways.

Pathways not only connect different destinations, they give artistic flow and an overall feel to a design. To create your pathways, I suggest you study, get inspired by, and directly imitate patterns in nature. Imitating patterns in nature creates life in the same way nature creates life. Nature is the grand designer for maximizing life and so what works for her is likely to work best for us in creating outdoor spaces.

In observing nature, we notice she uses many patterns again and again, from microcosm to macrocosm: spirals, double spirals, triple spirals, ripples, flow forms, roots and branches, bee-hives, ebbs and flows, waves, explosions, mushrooms, petals, hearts, tear drops, coils, keyholes, etc. In this section, we will look at the practical benefits of employing these patterns in your home farm. We'll see why people resonate with these patterns. And we'll explore how you can decide which pattern or patterns are right for you personally to use on your home farm.

Photograph 3.9 Imitating Patterns in Nature - Peg and Charlie Galbraith Gardens

Drawing 3.3 Common Patterns in Nature

Practically speaking, paths must get us somewhere we want to go and keep us out of places we shouldn't go (in the soil of growing beds, for example). In a small, active space, destinations abound. Branches, spirals, and loops all help the gardener access many different locations in a single pathway design and reach into lots of growing space without stepping on and compacting growing beds.

Patterns in nature always work to **increase edge effect,** another practical benefit to incorporating them into pathway design. The **edge effect** is a law of nature that asserts the interface, or edge, between two ecosystems creates a third, more complex system that combines elements of both. The edge offers a higher bio-diversity than either of the two areas that meet to create it. In nature, the interface receives more light and nutrients, and so is more productive. For example, where the high desert meets the Rio Grande in the corner of the world where I live, we find the bosque, or the riparian zone. This is certainly a thoroughfare of wildlife and diversity, an ecosystem on which our human community greatly depends. Nature meanders the river back and forth in playful ribbons of water, increasing edge effect, thereby increasing life capacity.

In our outdoor spaces, we find edge between the house and gardens, animal shelters and surrounding areas, and human spaces in the garden (paths and outdoor living areas), as well as plant spaces (growing beds and food forests). We can increase the edge effect in our garden by ridding it of straight lines and meandering the paths to form a wheel, an S curve, or a figure 8. The floor of your patio can form a circle, a mushroom, or flower petals. Spend extra time in nature as you contemplate your design and see how she inspires you with her patterns.

Although straight lines are rare in nature, when we walk from point A to point B we tend to follow the quickest path, which is a straight line. You can include portions of this type of "path of least resistance" into your design without making the overall path a straight line. At Mother Nature Gardens, the longest, most frequently used path from the house to the straw bale shed is 3 to 4 feet wide and has a gentle curve in it. When I'm in a real rush, I can cut enough steps off my walk that I don't ever jump off the path to get to my destination. If I step off a path to get to my destination for any reason, the pathway loses its practicality. In pathways, form always follows function.

It's clear that patterns in nature have practical benefits but that's not my favorite reason for using them. These patterns resonate with people on a deep, instinctive level, that happy place where we are all one and integrated with life, nature, and each other. The human species has evolved in close connection with these patterns. Natural patterns of time form our calendars and festivals. Our bodies follow universal patterns of proportions. The systems that make up our bodies, our cells, and even our genes, follow natural patterns that divide like fractals into smaller but identical patterns.

My favorite example can be seen in our circulatory system. If you took a person's circulatory system – working inward from capillaries to veins to the heart center and then back out again through the artery system to the capillaries in our lungs – enlarged it and laid it out flat, it would look exactly like the branches and the roots of a tree. If you enlarged it even more, you might recognize it as a watershed. Tiny contributing streams come together in small rivers, into the main waterway and branch back out again into a delta before flowing into the ocean. We can't help but feel a connection to these forms because these patterns exist both within our bodies and everywhere in the world around us. They are the foundation of life – and we are joyously alive. So even if we are oblivious to these patterns on a conscious level, on some deeper level we resonate with them strongly.

Now, with all these different patterns that exist in the abundant world, which one is right for incorporating into the design of your home farm? Look at what you already have on your property. There are established pathways, and there are pathways that connect your desired farm elements. A pattern may very well be forming itself. I like when this happens in the design process because it feels like the land is asserting itself and expressing the pattern it wants to express. You may not experience that exactly, however, and that's fine. You may see a bit of a pattern but have to tweak a farm element placement a little to complete it. A pattern that resonates with you personally may be the first thing you come up with, and farm element placement may follow that pattern. If you feel most at home in the woods, create a trunk and branch pathway. If you live in the desert and yearn for the ocean, make a wave pattern. This will strengthen your connection with the space and draw you out into it more often. When winter comes and the green growth dies back, the art of the pathway comes to the forefront. If no particular pattern feels natural, just be inspired by nature and make your pathways flow, arch, and branch. If your design feels inspired, it probably is. The land wants to heal and wants to communicate with us. And I believe using natural patterns in the garden is a way of meeting the land half way. Using patterns from nature is one way that we help to bring all of our intentions for our home farm into alignment.

Our Home Farms
From Melanie

When we started looking at the pathways in my backyard, we knew a fruit tree would go back in one corner eventually and that the bees would be over there, and the chickens over there. We knew we were going to have to go back and forth from the tool shed a lot. After these practical considerations, we listened to our intuition in establishing a design. What Zoe came up with was the sacred heart pattern which is made up of two mirrored, connecting hearts, with a Star of David where the two hearts intersect at their bases. When she called me to tell me about her idea for the design I got very excited and the name for the design emerged to be Sacred Heart Backyard Farm.

 ## Think Big, Start Small

At this point in the chapter, your design may be fairly complete. I am sure it is a beautiful piece on paper. But what do you do now? Well, you certainly can't implement all your ideals immediately. The home farm is always in a state of becoming. It is immensely helpful to begin with an overall design that embodies your goal. However, transforming barren land into a thriving home farm takes years of labor, and gathering materials and resources along the way. The timeline varies considerably depending on how much time and/or money you have to invest in the project.

As a landscaper, after the time-intensive processes of design and planning for materials, our company can do in a week on someone else's property what has taken us years to do in our own yard. The difference is a considerable price tag. If you decide to work with a contractor, they need to have a clear idea of what you want done. Even if someone else will do much of the work, you need a plan. Get an idea of how the contractor incorporates sustainability into their work and determine if they are listening to you or not.

Most of us cannot afford immediate transformation to accomplish all we hope for. So, for the do-it-yourselfers, begin with the garden bed closest to your back door and extend out from there in concentric rings. Work in and fill up your inner ring first, before moving to the next ring of space. Remember, it's important as you add features not to block access to areas you plan to develop later.

By starting small you will quickly see what works and what doesn't. If you make a small mistake then you can learn from it instead of paying for it. With small steps you also don't have to spend much money, since you can organize small work parties and create simple earthworks on the weekend.

 Exercise 3.2

- *Make a three-year plan.* List goals by year. What in the grand plan can be done this year?

- *Give your plan a budget.* Estimate the cost of each investment item.

- *Plan your labor.* Intelligent labor is more valuable than brute force labor.

- *Refer to your list of materials needed.* Think about costs or time to acquire materials.

- *Adapt your design from the lesson of each new experience.* Sustainability is always in a state of becoming: becoming more efficient; becoming more alive; and becoming more integrated with your life as a homeowner or resident. Implementing sustainable practices stimulates new ideas unique to your property and circumstances.

section 2
The Infrastructure

On your home farm, infrastructure means the skeleton and hardware of how things work and grow. This includes outdoor living spaces and how water is captured, accessed, distributed, and re-used. The four chapters in this section will help you consider where water will come from to nourish your plants, and how this water can be used most safely and efficiently. You will also learn how to create outdoor living spaces that are enjoyable and appropriate for your needs and lifestyle.

Chapter Four:

Outdoor Living Areas

Overview

We have established that including yourself as a part of the outdoor environment is an important part of a successful design. You are now a farm element. Like the other creatures on your site, you need a place to do your thing comfortably (as discussed in Chapter Two) – work, play, eat, pray – while enjoying protection from the sun, wind, and sometimes rain and snow. You can accommodate all of these needs with outdoor living areas, extending the square footage of your home into your yard. In this chapter, we will look at various examples of outdoor living spaces.

Different types of living spaces are attractive and appropriate for different people. As you read through these ideas, think about which ones you would most like to implement. Tailor your outdoor living spaces to you, so they will get used. First, we will explore ways to stack outdoor living area functions to get the most out of this space. (Recall that in Chapter Three, we discussed the permaculture concept of stacking functions. This concept is important for all aspects of home farm planning, not just for how you locate your plants.) Then, we will look at examples of outdoor living areas. Because many of the suggested outdoor living areas include water use and thus, water waste, we will look at how to deposit greywater properly in the garden. Finally, we will introduce you to and describe how to make a grape ramada, a simple but beautiful shade structure to help you create an outdoor living area.

Stacking Functions of Your Outdoor Living Space

 ## Shade Structures

When possible, outdoor living areas should double as shade structures for the east/northeast and west/northwest sides of your home. This way, they stack functions by providing places to work and relax, while helping to control indoor temperatures passively. This also assures that the outdoor space is close to the indoor space, increasing its accessibility.

Photograph 4.1 Example of How a Shade Structure Provides Shade to the Garden as well as the People – Courtesy of Sherry Smith

Shade structures can also offer partial shade to adjacent growing areas. The beds benefit from the same protection we grant ourselves. Vines planted in growing beds can use the shade structure for support. Shade structures also help protect house foundations. Irrigating within 4 feet of the house can compromise its foundations. Outdoor living areas adjacent to the home can create a safety gap between the home's foundation and watered beds.

Greywater Use

Outdoor living spaces often have water features: an outdoor sink to wash veggies; an outdoor washing machine right next to your clothes line; or an outdoor shower tucked into a "bamboo forest" for privacy. Outdoor living spaces can also provide opportunities to utilize greywater without ever having to drill a hole in your exterior wall or investigate a crawl space. Greywater is water you use once in your home that can safely be used again for another purpose. For example, water used to rinse off vegetables can be used again to water your garden. By creating household areas where you use water outside, you have the opportunity for the simplest greywater system and, just as importantly, you spend time in your garden observing and connecting with your environment. For example, wastewater from an outdoor washing machine can be channeled into your garden and used to water fruit trees or to go into surge basins. For this type of greywater use, it's important that only safe detergents are used to wash your clothes (see "How to Discharge Greywater Properly" on page 124 in this chapter), and that the water has not been used for clothing saturated with biological or chemical waste, like soiled diapers or clothing worn around chemicals.

Catch More Rainwater

When outdoor living areas are covered with solid roofing like sheets of corrugated steel, they offer another surface from which to collect water. Angle the roof to flow directly into a growing bed. Alternately, gutter the roof so water flows into a rainwater barrel.

Types of Outdoor Living Areas

 ## Outdoor Eating and Entertaining

Growing up, my family and I gathered around a picnic table every summer evening, eating corn on the cob from the garden and waiting to see the first lightning bugs for the night. I enjoy those memories of unity and connection from my childhood. Shaded by a tree or a gazebo, outdoor tables make great places to connect with nature over a meal. If you have a tree that makes it difficult to grow plants in a certain area, but you don't want to part with its shade, turn the space under the tree into an eating area. Remember, birds also love trees, so have a cover to protect your table from droppings when you are not using it. Outdoor tables can double as outdoor desks for reading or journaling. hayneedle.com is a good source for outdoor living area supplies and furniture.

Photograph 4.2 Children Love Outdoor Eating/Entertaining Areas

Outdoor Meditation Areas

Many people go to their gardens for spiritual connection. Green growth, birds, and butterflies help us return to a moment of wonder and gratitude and remember the divine, by whatever name. A beautifully-placed bench in a well-arranged area in the garden offers an ideal spot to sit and reflect or just be present in the moment.

Think about where best to place this area. When will you use it? I have a seat facing the southeast because I especially love to sit in direct sunlight in the morning. If you tend to meditate in the afternoons after work, you need an area shaded from the west. What do you want to look at? Not your neighbor's collection of random wire and wood (or yours for that matter). Is there a beautiful tree to gaze at or a mountain view? What functions do you want the area to perform for you? While public gathering areas work well as the focal point of a landscape, meditation areas feel more intimate when they are slightly hidden, tucked away behind plantings, a curve in the path, or an arbor.

 ## Outdoor Grill Area/Fire Pits

Fire makes people gather together, whether they are talking or singing around an outdoor fire with a hot cup of cider warming their hands in the fall, or chumming with the grill cook on a summer evening with an iced tea or cold beer. Having a counter and a little grill outdoors gives a whole new light to cooking – sunlight. While you prepare, cook, and clean, you share that sunlight with your garden plants and all the other creatures that are making their living on your land. Outdoor kitchens are common throughout central Africa and most tropical places, and we even had one in the 100-year-old Illinois farmhouse where I grew up. Keep your house cool in the summer and cook outdoors!

Outdoor grills and fire pits can vary considerably in detail and design. Decide if this is a winter or summer spot, or both, as that will affect your placement. Grills and fire pits need to be protected from the wind for the safest use of fire. At Mother Nature Gardens, we have a shade structure off the east side of our strawbale shed. We placed our grill right there. Then, we rescued a great '70s style leather couch from a street curb and put it right next to the grill. This makes a great place for guests to relax, look at our gardens, and chat with the grill chef. For some fun outdoor fire pit grill and kitchen area ideas, visit outdoorrooms.com.

Photograph 4.3
Outdoor Grill/Fire Pit

Outdoor Work Areas

Your needs from an outdoor work area will vary depending on the work you do. A shaded table where you can sit or stand up to work comfortably is the basic requirement for outdoor potting, crafting, cleaning, sawing, monkey-wrenching, tinkering, or leather tanning. Some work areas change with the season. For example, we have an open spot where I work with the bees in the spring and summer and chop and store wood in the fall and winter.

Outdoor Washing Areas

The greywater suggestions in this chapter are related to using outdoor washing machines, sinks, and showers. We use greywater as a way to get you outdoors instead of piping your indoor life outside. To get greywater from the inside of the house to outdoor distribution systems requires only a few more steps than a greywater system that begins outdoors, but one of those steps requires putting a hole in your wall. That, we feel, is beyond the scope of this book and is often beyond the capacity of the typical do-it-yourselfer. Of course, these systems are seasonal. Unless you live in the few places in the US that don't freeze in the winter, you will have to turn water valves off before a first freeze and then move your work indoors. For my situation, the time and energy required to make this seasonal shift is compensated by the simplicity and affordability of installing one of these outdoor greywater systems.

Please note that there are specific legal, technical requirements for installing complete greywater systems correctly. In this book we just want to introduce you to the idea and get you thinking about how you can use water most efficiently and creatively, although we will go into some of these considerations later in this chapter. If you want more in-depth information about greywater systems, we suggest greywater guru Art Ludwig's website, oasisdesign.net/greywater/laundry and his book, *The New Create an Oasis with Greywater*. Brad Lancaster's book, *Rainwater Harvesting for Drylands and Beyond Volume 2*, also addresses greywater considerations that are beyond the scope of this book.

At Mother Nature Gardens, our eight-inch crawl space made installing a greywater system unfeasible. As a compromise, we bring our washing machine outside during the spring, summer, and fall.

Over the past couple of years we have built a patio on the west side of the house, and this is where our washing machine is located when it is outdoors. A brick floor in this patio area, slightly canted away from our home, makes a clean, dry place for sitting. The shade structure Bard built as part of this patio provides hours of extra shade on the west side of our home during blazing summer afternoons. This has a huge impact on the temperature inside the house. Our office on the other side of that wall stays cool long into the afternoons. This extra protection from the heat allows us to use our swamp cooler (a type of home cooling unit used in the Southwest) for only one or two months each summer. If you've ever been to Albuquerque in May-August, you'll know this is a big deal.

Photograph 4.4 Outdoor Laundry

We place our washing machine outside on cement blocks to give it a stronger gravity drain. They set up a simple greywater system that deposits the water from the washing machine in four different deposit basins, each containing a valve that allows us to shut off a station if we wish (see section "How to Properly Discharge Greywater Properly" later in this chapter for details on creating this system for yourself). We also modified this system so that I could drain the machine into the sewer when I washed diapers or had other wash cycles that we didn't want to drain into the garden. We switched our soaps to those that were free of dioxane phospate, formaldehyde, and petrochemicals so our gardens wouldn't absorb these harsh pollutants. In making these choices, we saved our own skin and the watershed from exposure to the same harmful chemicals.

I enjoy doing my laundry outside. I like watching the gardens, chickens, birds, and butterflies while I wash. I can also be outside with my son while he plays. And I know that the draining water supports the life around me. When I take out a load of wash, I simply turn around to hang it in the sun to dry.

In the late fall, we move the washer back inside before the first hard frost sets in. We hope to close in our westside patio area with plastic walls for the coming winter so we can keep our washing machine in this area year-round, while creating a heat generator against our house to help with heating costs. Another idea for not having to move your washing machine twice a year is to acquire a second one (so there is an indoor and outdoor machine) or commit to using a laundromat during winter months.

Outdoor Showers

Refresh yourself in the summer heat with an outdoor shower and water your plants at the same time. For a semi-permanent shower, you will need a floor that drains, shelter, a hose with a spray nozzle (look for nozzles with convenient shut-off valves), and a stand to throw your hose over. If you would like your shower water to be warm, you may want to research and install a solar shower. We have used one that is a simple black plastic bag with a connecting hose and an on/off valve. Make these components as simple or as elaborate as you wish. Like everything else on your farm, it will develop over time.

Photograph 4.5 Bard Tests the Outdoor Shower

For your outdoor shower platform, you can create a sloped floor with paving stones that slant toward your plants. Alternately, cant the soil beneath the shower and make a floor of well-spaced wooden planks. Both of these methods will help you keep your feet clean while bathing. Create walls with any type of fencing material. While traveling in different developing countries, I have noticed a simple spiral shower pattern used again and again. The spiral creates an entrance as well as full privacy for bathers and requires very few carpentry skills.

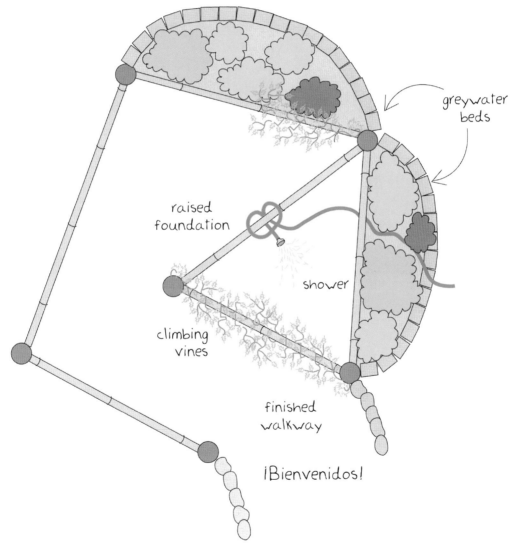

Drawing 4.1 Spiral Shower

Here are the basic steps to build a spiral shower:

1. Create your platform that will shed water to your designated planted area.

2. Bury 5- to 7-foot fence posts (wood or metal will do) to frame the spiral. These need to be tall enough to hide you within. You're not constructing anything that is going to hold a roof so even a 4-inch diameter pole will hold up a spiral fence. Because this area will likely be wet, treat around the bottom of wooden posts with linseed oil or drop them in concrete to increase the shower's lifespan. Your entrance to the shower is the outside of the spiral.

3. Make two opposing poles higher than the rest. These posts will support your crossbeam for hanging your hose shower. This step may not be necessary if you chose tall posts for the entire spiral.

4. Wire or screw a crossbeam to the top of each of the tall poles. Ensure that this crossbeam can hold the weight of a hose. This is your hose bar.

5. Then, tie reed fencing to the poles. Add as much fencing as you need to provide sufficient privacy for your outdoor shower. Plant vine climbers to increase your privacy and add to the romantic aesthetic of showering outdoors.

This is one easy, inexpensive idea but there is no limit to the creative design or materials you can use to build an outside shower. The only standards you need are a sloped floor that diverts the water to where it will be most beneficial, and privacy so bathers enjoy their time outdoors.

How to Discharge Greywater Properly

The most important thing to consider when using greywater is how to discharge it properly. Greywater may contain bacteria washed from your body, clothes, or food. Because of this, the following greywater do's and don'ts assure garden and homeowner health:

• Do avoid direct physical contact with greywater. Don't let children make mud pies with greywater-soaked soil, or allow pets to drink from the pooled water.

• Do discharge the water below the surface of the ground. Cover greywater tube openings with a couple inches of mulch within the infiltration basin. (We will give more information about infiltration basins below in this chapter.)

- Do not allow greywater to come into contact with edible portions of food crops like root crops or low-growing edibles like salad greens or strawberries. Instead, use greywater to water fruit and nut trees or vegetables with high-growing fruit like stalked tomatoes, artichokes, or berry bushes. The plant itself will act as a secondary filter for the greywater. The infiltration basin is your first filter.

- Do make sure there is significant space to distribute the greywater. Never let greywater pool in your garden or waterlog soil for more than 24 hours. This often requires having multiple, properly mulched distribution basins as well as a sewer outlet so you can direct the water to different areas for absorption or disposal as appropriate.

- Do plant trees and perennials around infiltration basins to help pull water below the soil surface quickly.

- Don't store greywater in barrels. Organic materials in greywater decompose quickly and make a foul odor.

- Don't use harsh chemicals in washing that can harm your plants. If you wish to recycle your greywater, you must become aware of harmful ingredients found in detergents and soaps. This is a great example of co-healing with the earth. As we eliminate harsh soaps to protect our plants' health, we improve our own health simultaneously. Some soaps are advertised as being "greywater safe." Nonetheless, scan the ingredients to avoid any of the following (list compiled from harvestingrainwater.com):

  - Chlorine, bleach, and fabric softeners;

  - Detergents with whiteners, softeners, and enzymes;

  - Sodium-based detergents;

  - Boron. This is considered a plant nutrient but is required only in very, very small amounts;

  - Soaps and detergents with the following ingredients: peroxygen, sodium perborate, sodium trypochlorite, petroleum distillate, alkylbenzene, and salt; and

  - Disinfectants.

- Always reserve the option to drain your greywater into the sewer. When your mulch basins are saturated, when you wash dirty diapers or clothes worn by someone with an infectious disease, or when you run out of your new clean soap and are using your old soap just until you get to the store, always have easy access to the sewer line.

- Do flush out your mulch basins periodically with rainwater. Greywater is typically alkaline and contains salts that build up easily in desert soil. Rainwater cleanses the area and helps avoid salt build-up.

- Do add white vinegar periodically to your greywater where it is discharged to help lower or neutralize the pH of your water.

Making a Greywater Infiltration Basin

An infiltration basin is an area that is used to filter greywater quickly and efficiently. Infiltration basins, which are essential to filtering organic matter and soaps from greywater quickly and efficiently, are simple, inexpensive, and as effective as sewer treatment plants. An infiltration basin is similar to the sponges described in Chapter Three (that is, a large hole filled with mulch, straw, or other organic matter), except that an infiltration basin is larger and has a subsurface inlet pipe. Within the mulched basin is a void space, creating by an upside down 5-gallon bucket with a hole in the side to receive the inlet pipe, or a rock-lined basin that keeps the mulch from backfilling. This void space holds a surge of greywater below the earth's surface until the mulch around it can absorb it. Cover the void with a wide rock.

1. Size mulched basins to handle one to one-and-a-half times the peak greywater surge. An old-school washing machine will discharge 40 gallons of water for every load, distributed in two halves. So the basin for an outdoor washing machine should hold at least 20 gallons of water. If you have very clay-based soil, the water will soak in slowly between rinses, so increase your peak surge capacity to 30 gallons. If your system deposits into several basins simultaneously, your basins should hold a cumulative peak surge.

2. Soak your site with water to facilitate digging, and then dig, baby, dig!

3. Backfill the basin with compacted organic material: wood chips, straw (leave it compacted from the bale if possible), manure, newspapers, or old phone books.

4. In the center of the basin, install your upside down, 5-gallon bucket with a hole to fit the inlet pipe, or a circular rock wall set 18 inches down into the soil.

Now that you have a place to receive water, you are ready to connect your source and your outlet. At Mother Nature Gardens we used 1.5-inch PVC piping laid on a 2% slope from the washing machine to our basins. We have four infiltration basins attached to the same pipe leading to the washing machine. Each outlet has a turn-off valve so we can control how much water each area receives. Alternately, you can install multiple PVC pipes that all begin at the washing machine outlet. To move the water around to different areas in this system, you switch the washing machine outlet pipe to the different PVC pipes. This method works well if you want to move the water around to widely dispersed areas in your yard, whereas the setup at Mother Nature Gardens has a fairly narrow channel of water distribution.

Photograph 4.6 Infiltration Basin without Sides

Photograph 4.7 Infiltration Basin with Sides

Photograph 4.8 Pipes
Going from a Washing
Machine to a Series of
Basins

Grape Ramada/Shade Structure

A grape ramada is a simple structure made from either rough-cut lumber, recycled wood, or pine or juniper poles. The goal is to create shade while providing a support for growing grapes (lovers of hot sun and poor soil). Two to four grape plants of different varieties can grow on a ramada. The grapes provide food, shade, and greenery for the homeowner. The shade structure can host any of the outdoor living activities mentioned previously, as well as additional activities you have thought of that we haven't.

Photograph 4.9 Grape Ramada

A basic ramada measures 10 feet square. Make the roof from 12-foot latillas (rough, round branches that are peeled or unpeeled, depending on your taste). The roof can slope in any direction. When building, take into consideration what time of day you mostly plan to use this area. If you use it in the afternoon, you don't want it to be open to the west. Make the roof tall enough for your tallest family member or friend to stand comfortably, but not so tall that the grapes are out of reach.

Create a flat, raised area for the floor. There are many options for floor materials: brick, flagstone, cobblestone, crusher fine, or even mulch.

 Exercise 4.1

1. Which of the following elements do you want to include in your home farm?

   - A shade structure
   - A greywater system
   - An outdoor eating or entertaining area
   - An outdoor grill area or fire pit
   - A meditation area
   - An outdoor work area
   - An outdoor laundry area and/or sink
   - An outdoor shower
   - A grape ramada

2. Mark on your site plan where each of these might be located.

Chapter Five:

Active Rainwater Harvesting

Overview

Active rainwater harvesting catches roof run-off water (from snow melt, little sprinkles, and big storms) in barrels or cisterns for irrigation during dry periods. Rainwater does not contain the salts and chlorine of city water, nor the chemical run-off or weed seeds of water that is available in some areas through traditional irrigation ditches, called *acequias*. Furthermore, rainwater gathers nitrogen in the air as it falls to the ground, so it fertilizes the soil while giving it water. Catching rainwater increases our natural growing capacity with a completely renewable, clean, and, after the initial investment, free water source. Using rainwater to irrigate ties us closer to the source of our water. When you irrigate with rainwater, you become even more grateful for the rain and begin to determine how to live within your rainwater budget. Two excellent resources to learn more about rainwater harvesting are *'Rainwater Harvesting for Drylands and Beyond Volume 2'* by Brad Lancaster and *'Harvest the Rain'* by Nate Downey.

Both of these will ideally be hotlinked to Amazon.com through my affiliate setup.

At Mother Nature Gardens, we harvest rainwater in a 2,900—gallon cement cistern as well as multiple polyurethane tanks. Bard installed all of them as well as dozens more around our city. In this chapter, Bard helped us form a step-by-step guide for readers to create their own off-the-grid watering system.

To get started, we will determine the size of the tanks appropriate for you and your space. We'll briefly look at different types of rainwater tanks and cisterns. Then we'll look at the ideal location on your property to place your cistern or cisterns. Finally, we'll give you a set of steps for installing your tank or tanks.

Helpful Notes: Concerns about Toxins in Harvested Rainwater

Drylands Permaculture expert Jim Brookes, owner of Soilutions in Albuquerque, NM, soilutions.net, addresses concerns about collecting water from roofs and the fear that toxins could leach into the soil and be taken up by fruits and vegetables:

"In the concern over the quality of storm water runoff from roofs, the primary issue is hydrocarbons that may leach from roof materials, and those have been extensively studied. The bottom line is that as long as the soil pH is in the normally accepted range for growing food crops, and there is adequate microbiological activity in the soil, then there is very little risk of hydrocarbon buildup in the soil. The hydrocarbons are consumed readily as a food source for the microbes. And, the minerals that are represented in these hydrocarbon compounds are bound up in the humus matrix and then taken up by plants as needed for their cellular health.

"Runoff from metal roofs is sometimes a concern due to zinc. While microbes don't readily consume zinc, they do effectively bind it into the organic matrix in humus or other organic complexes, thus preventing it from becoming water-soluble, even as it remains available for use by the plants as needed.

"So, although I probably would not choose to drink water directly coming from composite roofs (unless I was really thirsty), I would not hesitate to use it on crops. After all, the microbes need to have something to eat for energy and I'd rather have my soils treat the contamination before that water gets concentrated in the river."

Determine How Much Water Storage is Needed

Jim Brookes also reminds us to "prepare for the surge." When people ask him, "How big should my water tank be?" he answers with another question, "How big do you want your savings account to be?" The answer to that is always, "Big." You don't want your savings account limited. It's the same with water storage. We're only as water rich as our capacity to catch and keep water.

Another common question when it comes to rainwater harvesting is, "Do we really get enough rain in the drylands for rainwater harvesting to be worth it?" So without further ado, let's look at the following equation.

Calculation for Water Catchment Capacity:

For every 1,000 square feet of roof space, you can harvest 500 gallons (flat roof) to 600 gallons (pitched metal roof) for every one inch of rainfall. In Albuquerque, a city in the desert, our average eight inches of yearly rainfall yields 4,000 to 4,800 gallons of water a year from a 1,000 square foot roof.

What a capacity for plenty! The roof is such a large component of our modern properties that for most of us we could easily double the annual rainfall on our green spaces within the city if we caught and redistributed roof water run-off. It's exciting to realize rainwater could almost completely sustain home farm cultivation. For me, just thinking about it feels like the charged air right before a rainstorm.

Arid climates with a rainy season are ideal for large-capacity rainwater catchment. Of the eight inches of annual rainfall we typically receive in Albuquerque, several inches fall quite fiercely during the monsoon season, which is usually sometime in July through August. We hope for wet winters, get a little rain in the spring, and then hold on through the heat of summer until the monsoons come. Monsoon rains dump large quantities of water in a short time. So a 50-gallon drum beneath the canale or downspout in a surging downpour, fills instantly. Once the monsoons pass and we start the extensive dry period, that same drum empties in a flash. If we prepare for large-capacity storage, we can hold all the rain that falls during a powerful storm.

Exercise 5.1 Calculating Your Annual Rainwater Harvesting Potential

Here are steps for calculating how much water you could possibly harvest off the roofs on your property:

1. Find out the average annual rainfall in your city or town. This is easy to do by searching for this information on the Internet.

2. Use a site plan for your home to calculate the square footage of roof space you have. If you do not have a site plan, do a quick drawing of your home, and measure the roof area. The most accurate way to do this is to go up on the roof and measure it (only if its flat, of course), but you can get a rough estimate by measuring the eaves of the house.

3. Observe how much water flows out of each canale or gutter. Don't assume they all flow evenly or at all. Watch during a storm. Check the ground after a storm for water damage. If you have a flat roof and are able, climb a ladder and look at your roof. There are no standards for how to drain water off a flat roof and so you can find all kinds of oddities with a bird's eye view.

4. If you have a flat roof, calculate your annual rainwater harvesting potential using this formula:

    _____ (average annual rainfall in inches) x _____ (square footage of roof) x 500 gallons/1,000 square feet =

    If you have a pitched roof, calculate your annual rainwater harvesting potential using this formula:

    _____ (average annual rainfall in inches) x _____ (square footage of roof) x 600 gallons/1,000 square feet =

Types of Cisterns

 ## High-density Plastic Tanks

Plastic cisterns are the most cost-effective tanks to install. They are high-density, black polyethylene tanks that resist algae growth and are available in sizes ranging from 100 to 10,000 gallons. These tanks come with a filter basket at the inlet to catch debris that flow from the roof. Installation is easy. Just clear a flat area (slightly raised from the surrounding area), set it down, and connect it to the guttering system. If you move homes in the future, you can move the tank with you. The main stumbling block for most people is the aesthetics of the plastic tanks. However, you can easily paint, fence, or cover your tank with trellises and vines. The tanks also come in a variety of shapes, allowing you to choose the most discreet for your site.

In this book, as in the work we do in our sustainable landscaping company, we focus on this type of tank because it is affordable, portable, and simple enough for many homeowners to install successfully. Our company most commonly installs 550- and 1,000-gallon tanks that are tall with a relatively small footprint (just under four feet).

Photograph 5.1 High Density Plastic Tank

Ferrocement (Concrete)

Ferrocement tanks are made of rebar-reinforced walls plastered with concrete, and they give builders a lot of freedom to design for each unique location. You can paint or plaster a ferrocement tank the same color as your house, which allows it to blend in easily. And although labor is very costly for building these tanks, material costs are low. This makes ferrocement a good choice for skilled, do-it-yourself home farmers, as well as developing nations.

Some of the disadvantages of ferrocement tanks include: difficulties in building (especially when done without experience); high cost per gallon (if you hire someone else to do it for you); and leaks. To seal a ferrocement tank properly requires several coats of sealant. Experience has shown us that the tanks may need to be resealed several times to prevent leaks. You can't take a ferrocement tank with you if you move, but its permanence could increase the resale value of your house. Resources needed to build a ferrocement tank include skilled labor, proper tools, plastering materials, lots of rebar, and water-proofing sealant.

 **Our Home Farms**
From Zoe

At Mother Nature Gardens we installed our prototype rainwater harvesting cistern soon after we started growing on our land. With the help of Jim Brookes and Soilutions, Bard designed and built a 2,900-gallon tank with foam-insulated panels. Cement plaster was then sprayed over the paneling.

It's a great tank that does not leak, but it will always stay with the house. Because of its permanence, we took plenty of time to place it properly. It shades the west side of the house and provides privacy from our neighbors. It's also a great platform to stand on and look for rain clouds.

The first season, the level of water in the tank stayed fairly low because of a dry winter. That spring, we had 2,500 gallons in the tank and it almost went dry in July. Our gardens were still small, but we were learning to use the rainwater properly.

Since then, we have added an additional 550-gallon tank to harvest rain off the 200–square-foot strawbale shed, a 125-gallon tank harvesting rain off the neighbor's house (we save their foundation from the previously pooling water, and they are happy about that), and a 55-gallon drum harvesting rain off the shade structure on the west side of our house. These new additions increase our capacity from 2,900 gallons to 3,630 gallons. The precipitation that fills our tanks from the monsoons through late winter now allows us to irrigate our large garden only with rainwater throughout the long hot springs and summers.

Photograph 5.2 Mother Nature Gardens Cistern

Placing the Cistern

To place the cistern properly, you have to bridge from the water source (gutter) to where you need the water to go (cistern) in the simplest way possible. Begin by knowing where you want the cistern to go. Then, find the nearest gutter or canale. Use a ladder to check how much roof space drains to that outlet. For a 550-gallon cistern, you need at least 250 square feet of roof space to harvest from. Four inches of rain will fill your tank.

You'll find that pitched roofs with gutters grant a lot more freedom for cistern placement than flat roofs with canales. Surprisingly, builders don't often consider the impact on the property of surging roof water, let alone how to harvest it. As a result, canales are often located in weird spots, like over a door, window, or sidewalk. Multiple canales create further collection challenges.

Here are a few solutions to awkward canale placement:

- You can run gutters between canales to a single tank (which creates a complex inlet but a simple outlet system). This makes sense if you want to automate your outlet system.

- Alternatively, you can have a multiple-tank system. So, instead of one very large tank, you can install several tall, slender tanks under multiple canales (simple inlet with a higher-maintenance outlet system).

- Or, you may choose to harvest actively from one canale while other gutters feed into a passive watering system of basins and stream beds.

Remember the concept of stacking functions when placing your cistern. One element supports many functions and one function supports many elements, so make your cistern perform multiple functions in your landscape. Use your cistern's shade, its capacity to block a view, its potential to function as a giant canvas, and even its height to your additional advantage. For example, one family we visited had their home on a hill. They placed their cistern downhill and made a patio over the top of it. They needed a pump to push the water out but they accomplished two results they valued, a completely disguised tank and a patio out their back door.

Most rainwater harvesters like the idea of disguising the tank. In our landscaping business, we often use several tall, slender cisterns versus one large one because they can easily be tucked behind corners and between windows. After proper placement, you can implement additional techniques for disguising your tanks. You can make an arbor supported by the tank or over it and use the tank to grow vegetables vertically. I like having shaded water sources because gardeners spend a lot of time at the watering hole. You can build a coyote fence (tightly juxtaposed aspen or pine poles) around cisterns, then grow vines on the fencing.

You can also go in the other direction with the aesthetics question and make your cistern a garden focal point. Cisterns provide an open canvas for murals. Ferrocement tanks hold outdoor concrete paint with ease. When painting a plastic tank, use an undercoat of plastic primer. Then use acrylic latex for your topcoat so the paint can expand and contract.

Installation

 ## Foundation

Once you have chosen the location for your cistern, clear the area. A 550-gallon cistern measures 4-feet in diameter by 76-inches tall. For a cistern of this size, you will need to clear an area 66 inches in diameter of all debris (including rocks, sticks, and nails). Raise the platform a couple of inches higher than the surrounding area and use a level to make the ground flat. Now, you are ready to install the tank.

 ## Gutters

The simplest gutter-to-cistern configuration places the cistern directly under the canale with one straight gutter from the canale to the cistern opening. Don't restrict yourself to this arrangement, however. A gutter (often with a trellis for aesthetics and additional support), can be installed as a bridge between your house and where you want to place your cistern.

At the roof's edge, attach the downspout to the gutter leading to your cistern. Use a saw to trim the gutter about 2 feet above the top of the cistern. Use a flexible downspout (a piece of plastic guttering that expands like an accordian) to attach the downspout to the cistern. Fasten it with sheet-metal screws. Seal any seams with caulk.

Of course, if you are not comfortable doing this yourself, or don't have time but can afford to pay someone to do this for you, you can always hire a contractor to help you with this installation.

Attaching a down spout to a canale requires a couple of additional steps. First, you must stop up the end of the canale. The best technique we've found is a glued and caulked piece of scrap metal, cut slightly wider than the opening, and bent so both sides curve inside the canale. Then, cut a hole in the bottom of the canale and attach the flexible downspout to the new opening. Seal this connection with caulk.

Screens

Multiple, well-placed, seasonally-maintained screens keep water flow through gutters clear. More than just water travels through these passageways. Screens keep organic matter, namely leaves, from flowing into your tank, which keeps tank water fresher longer. Gutter screens also prevent mice and other little critters from entering your water supply.

Install a piece of screen at the junction between the vertical and horizontal gutter and at the location where the gutter enters the tank, making sure all screens are accessible for cleaning. Clean gutter screens seasonally to prevent backups and overflows. "First flush" systems exist that do this job automatically, but they cost money to purchase and time to install.

Overflow

Since your tank may fill up at some point during the course of a year, you need a way for the tank to overflow. At the top of the tank, install a 2-inch overflow pipe. For the overflow, you will need a 2-inch bulkhead fitting. Ask the person that sells you the tank to install the bulkheads for you. Use 2 inches of PVC pipe to direct the overflow into a planted, depressed basin. Place a small piece of screen between one of the fittings on the overflow to keep mosquitoes from entering your cistern.

Photograph 5.3 Overflow on a 2900 gallon tank

Getting Water Out of Your Tank

 Gravity Feed Systems

It is possible to feed water out of your tank by gravity even on flat ground. Simply connect a hose to the outlet. However, placing your cistern high on a slope or elevating it on cement blocks will increase the pressure available from gravity, as will the amount of water you have in your tank – the more water in the tank, the more pressure available from gravity. Raising your tank also allows you to slip a watering can beneath your outlet. Gravity produces enough pressure for a hose but not enough to feed a drip irrigation system. Watering by gravity feed through a hose is a fallback method and should be available in addition to any other systems designed to pump water out of the tank.

Install the outlet 3 to 6 inches above the bottom of the cistern. This way, you do not pull from the bottom water, which may have debris in it. If your tank is not elevated, raise the outlet to 12 to 18 inches from the tank bottom in order to fit a watering can beneath. When you want to use that last bit of water, you'll need a sump pump to get it out. Make your outlet fit a standard hose bib. To install the hose bib you will need a ¾-inch bulkhead fitting and water-resistant sealant.

Helpful Notes: Tips for Irrigating with Rainwater:

- If the plant can't survive on the amount of rainwater available to water it, don't grow it.

- Mulch heavily, and irrigate underneath the mulch with drip irrigation. (We will explain how to do this below.)

- Water early in the morning or in the evening.

- Don't let the soil dry out too much between waterings.

- To see parts online, visit rainharvest.com, the largest inventory of rain harvesting systems internationally.

Drop-from-the-Top Pump

The next simplest method for getting your stored water out of the cistern is a drop-from-the-top submersible pump, which is what we have used successfully at Mother Nature Gardens for years. Plug in a sump-pump ($85-$100 at a hardware store) and connect it to a hose. We climb a ladder, open the tank lid, and drop our pump into the water. The outlet hose hooks up to the drip system and runs it for as long as we need. Once the pump gets started, it will continue to siphon, whether or not it remains plugged in. The siphoning doesn't stop when the electricity to the pump is cut, it only stops when the pump is removed from the water. One advantage of this is that you can turn the pump off shortly after turning it on and still water at a lower pressure when you want to. The disadvantage is, of course, unless you lift the pump out of the water, it will continue to drain your tank. This hands-on method clearly requires your presence to start and stop the system.

Automated Pump System

An automated system uses a sump pump equipped with a float that feeds a drip irrigation system. A timer turns the system on and off while the float prevents the pump from continually pumping the water out after the system turns off. It requires an electrical outlet. We describe a hand-engineered system below that Bard has tested with great results in medium-sized vegetable gardens (under 200 feet of in-line irrigation tubing). However, if you have more money than tolerance for home engineering your plumbing parts, Grundfos MQ makes a top-of-the-line, on-demand pump with a built-in pressure tank. Although it is pricey and still requires skill to install, this type of system can reliably irrigate large areas from the water stored in water tanks.

Photograph 5.4 Automated Pump System on a Rain Water Cistern

Helpful Notes: List of Materials for an Automated Pump System

Get all parts at a quality, local pump and pipe store. Local irrigation stores may also carry some of these parts.

- A water-proof outlet (preferably covered)
- 1" bulkhead fitting
- Sump pump with an attached float
- 1" clear tubing
- ½" reducer
- A cement block
- Hole saw
- Screening
- Caulk
- Grommet
- Teflon tape
- An outdoor timer
- AVB (Air Vacuum Breaker - we will describe the use for this below)
- PVC joint, 1" thread on one end, 1" slip on the other
- 1" T joint
- Two elbow joints
- PVC piping as tall as your pipe
- 1" female thread on the filter to a 3/4" pipe thread for the poly pipe.

(Please note: We know these next two sections may be way beyond anything you want to deal with. You *always* have the option of hiring a vendor. We provide this information for you in case it is an area of interest for you and you want to do it yourself, or you want to understand better what your contractor is doing so you can participate in the process in some capacity.)

To install your automated pump system:

1. Install a 1-inch bulkhead fitting on the side of the tank where you want the water to exit. Place the fitting high enough that you can comfortably reach inside from the top to unscrew the pipe and replace or remove the pump if needed. In a pumped system, the pump is at the bottom of the tank and pumps the water up through a tube in the tank, out a hole in the top of the tank, and back down through hard pipe on the outside of the tank.

2. Next, get your sump pump with a float. Attach 1-inch clear piping to the pump outlet. A sump pump outlet usually measures 1½ inches. Use a ½-inch reducer to reduce it to the necessary 1 inch.

3. The pump and float electrical cords require their own exit hole, located above the overflow. Bard typically uses a hole saw to drill the 2-inch hole as high on the manhole as possible. Run the cord out the exit hole before dropping the pump in the tank.

4. Screen and caulk around the hole to make it mosquito proof.

5. Use a rope to lower a cement block gently into the bottom of the tank.

6. Connect the clear 1-inch piping to the pump (this will connect to the 1-inch bulkhead water exit point). Seal connecting pieces with teflon tape.

7. Then, lower your pump into the tank by its cords, setting it on the cement block. Placing the pump on the cement block assures it won't pull dirty water from the bottom of the tank.

8. With the pump in place, connect the clear 1-inch piping from the pump to the bulkhead fitting. Be sure to use teflon tape on all fittings and you've completed the inside of the tank.

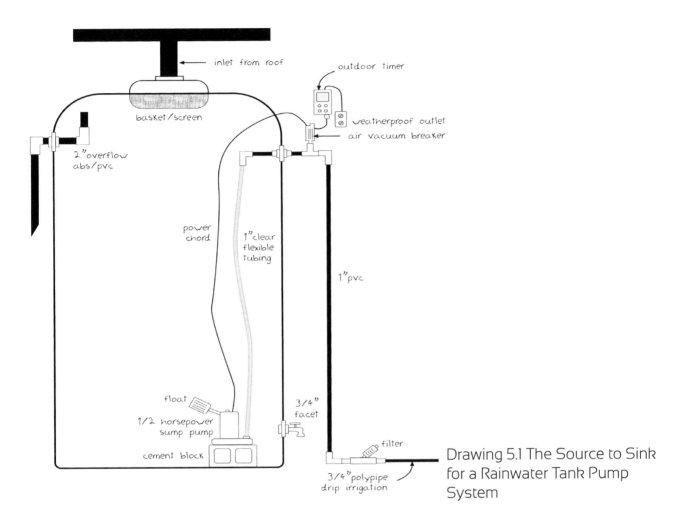

inlet from roof

outdoor timer

basket/screen

weatherproof outlet

air vacuum breaker

2"overflow
abs/pvc

power
chord

1"clear
flexible
tubing

1"pvc

float

3/4"
facet

1/2 horsepower
sump pump

cement block

filter

3/4"polypipe
drip irrigation

Drawing 5.1 The Source to Sink for a Rainwater Tank Pump System

Now, we'll walk through the tasks required for setting up the outside of the tank.

1. Install the air vacuum breaker (AVB) directly outside the water exit. An air vacuum breaker breaks the continual siphon that occurs with sump pumps by dropping an air pocket into the line after the electricity is cut off to the pump.

2. Thread a PVC joint to the bulkhead fitting, a 1-inch male thread by 1-inch slip. Use teflon on the threads.

3. Then, attach a 1-inch T joint with the leg of the T pointing straight up.

4. Glue these joints.

5. Install the AVB on the top of the T. You will need a 1-inch nipple to join the threaded adapter on top of the T to the AVB.

6. Once you have installed the AVB, run the 1-inch PVC from the T, elbowed down to the ground with another elbow at the ground level.

7. Then, install a filter to remove any debris from the water before it enters the drip system. Find a filter at your local irrigation store. Follow the arrows on the filter to make sure you install it in the right direction.

8. Then, step down from the 1-inch female thread on the filter to a ¾-inch pipe thread for the poly pipe.

9. Then use ¾-inch poly pipe for your drip irrigation mainline as ½ inch will reduce pressure too much. You will learn the parts of the irrigation system in Chapter Six.

10. Mount the outdoor timer near the outlet and plug the pump and float cords into the timer. This is the system control center, which we will also cover more in Chapter Six.

11. Test your system by turning the timer on to the manual setting. Let it run for 15 minutes. Make sure that the water reaches all the way to the end of the irrigation line, using your finger to test the soil below the surface. If it pumps poorly, check the 1-inch line from the pump to the bulkhead, making sure there are no kinks in the line.

12. To maintain the system, clean the filter out every month or more, depending on how clean your rainwater is. In the winter, Bard pulls out the filter and drains the lines so that nothing freezes and breaks.

Helpful Notes: Cistern Pump Hookup Parts List

Quantity	Part	Size	Where to buy
1	sump pump w/ float	½ hp	Hardware store
1	outdoor plug-in timer		Hardware store
1	1 ½" reducer 1" galvanized		Hardware store
1	1" clear pipe	8'	Hardware store
2	male thread compression fittings	1"	Hardware store
Bag	1" clamps		Hardware store
1	bulkhead fitting	1"	Pump and Pipe store
2	1" male thread to slip	1"	Hardware store
	1" T PVC	1"	Hardware store
	1" x 2" long nipple	1"	Hardware store
2	1" 90° elbow PVC	1"	Hardware store
	Air vacuum breaker	1"	Pump and Pipe store
	PVC pipe	1"	Hardware store
	1" slip reduce ¾" male thread		Pump and Pipe store
	Filter	1"	Irrigation store
	¾" slip female to ¾" male thread	¾"	Irrigation store
	poly pipe compression fitting	¾"	Irrigation store

Exercise 5.2 Rainwater Catchment on Your Property

1. Look at the site map for your property. Locate where your gutters and/or canales are on your roof or roofs.

2. What challenges currently exist on your property to setting up a rainwater catchment and distribution system? How might you overcome these? What additional canales, gutters, or connections between existing canales and gutters do you need to collect the rainwater that falls on your roof or roofs most efficiently?

3. If you were going to set up a rainwater catchment system, where would it be most logical to locate your cistern or cisterns? How large would you like them to be? What type of cistern or cisterns would you install?

4. How will you distribute the water from your cisterns? Will you use a gravity feed system or an automated pump? Where will you channel the water? Will you hire a vendor or do the work yourself? From the information in this chapter, what else do you need to consider or plan in order to set up a rainwater catchment and distribution system on your particular property?

Chapter Six:

Installing an Irrigation System

Overview: Why a Drip Irrigation System?

Drip irrigation systems save water because they deliver a slow, steady dose of water to each plant's root zone, dripped directly above and accumulating in the root area. The slow flow gives each drop time to sink into the ground before the next drop. All the water provided for the plant serves the plant, significantly reducing water lost to run-off and evaporation.

Any tree, shrub, or perennial should have drip emitters installed at the time of planting and regular watering should continue for at least three years. Plants respond positively to the regularity of irrigation. You will certainly notice this if you switch over from hand watering. The homeowner benefits as well from the switch. Plants grow month after month, sometimes with no effort from the homeowner.

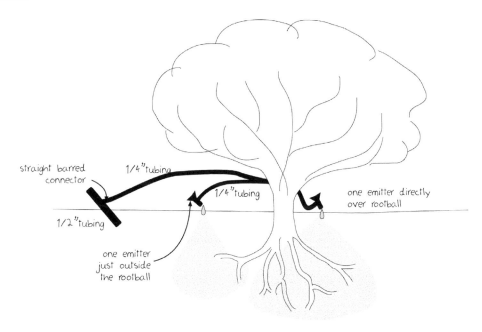

Drawing 6.1 Spread of Water Under an Emitter Around a Root Ball

There are different ways to install an irrigation system as well as different ways to distribute the water. In this chapter we provide a detailed introduction to drip irrigation systems so you can decide what type of system is right for you and potentially buy the parts as well as install it yourself. We answer questions of how much water to provide for different types and sizes of plants as well as when they should be watered. Finally, we lay out how to monitor your irrigation system so that plants get water only when they need it and the system stays functional year after year.

Two Types of Irrigation Systems Sources

The two types of irrigation system sources are a multiple ground zone system or a hose bib system. We will show you how to install a complete hose bib system and the second half of a multiple ground zone system. [*Please note:* After reading this chapter you may also decide to hire a contractor to install your irrigation system. This is fine! Understanding the overall functioning of an irrigation system will help you work more effectively with your contractor, get the best performance out of your irrigation system, and save money.] Always start with high quality irrigation parts from an irrigation store. This will save you maintenance in the future.

Many homes have some sort of irrigation system installed already at the time of purchase. If you have one, but question its quality or don't know where the lines are, spend some time to dig up the lines (mind the tree roots!) to see where they go. Map the system for future reference. When possible, identify and fix any leaks, and tap into the system you have now. Sometimes, however, after several homeowners or poor installation, systems get very complex and it can be best to start over.

Multiple Zones System

A zone is an area of land or type of vegetation that gets watered by one specific valve in a system of water valves. Each valve and zone in the system can have a different start time and watering duration.

Multiple-zone systems connect to city water valves, usually in a semi-buried, plastic box near the house. This system is controlled from a timer usually found in the garage or on the side or back of the house. Multiple-zone systems have a higher initial cost but last longer and have fewer maintenance issues. They allow you to address differences in watering needs with their different zones. Trees and many shrubs need infrequent, deep watering. Some shrubs and flowers need frequent, less-deep watering. Veggies need frequent, shallow watering. With a separate zone for each of these, you meet all needs simultaneously. In this type of system, different parts of the yard are often divided into sections.

On the down side, multiple-zone systems require a licensed plumber to install and are costly (expect a $1,500 starting cost). They also depend on city or well water. If you choose this type of system, let professionals install at least the valves, timer, and main lines for you. In this chapter, you will learn how to tap into your system to expand it, change it, or repair it.

Photograph 6.1 Multiple Zone System

Hose Bib System

A hose bib system is a simple, one-zone system. You attach a timer to your water source (your city or well water outlet or your cistern outlet) and irrigation piping or a hose/soaker hose to the timer. They are very easy and cost-efficient to install. However, this simple system is limited to one zone that waters everything for the same amount of time. To distribute different amounts of water to different plants, you will need to use emitters of different sizes. (We will explain below what emitters are, how they are sized, and why you will likely want to use emitters of different sizes.) Problems often arise with the timer for this type of system. Since the electrical box is in such close proximity to water, it is not uncommon for the box to short out. Also, you must dismantle this system in the winter to prevent freezing water from cracking the valves.

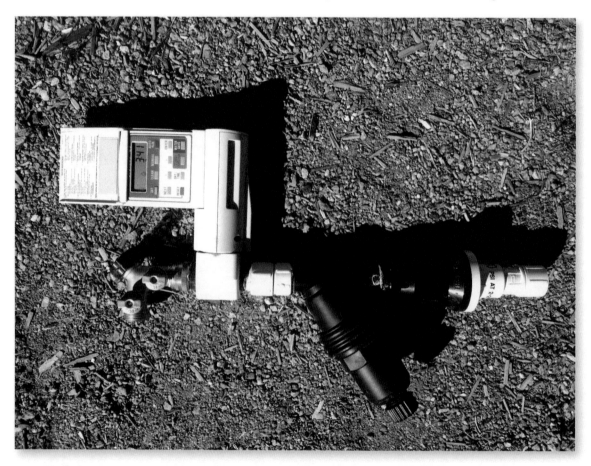

Photograph 6.2 From Top to Bottom - Timer, Brass Y, filter, pressure reducer, coupler.

Timer

A timer allows either type of irrigation system to monitor itself for extended periods of time. It is important to get comfortable with your timer and the timer manual, which will give step-by-step instructions for different functions. You will want to know how to turn the system on and off, how to change watering times for each zone, and how to turn the system on manually for emitter maintenance (see *Irrigation System Maintenance* below in this chapter).

When installing a timer at the hose valve, you may need an extension hose to fit everything in the small available space around the hose valve. If so, use a metal washing machine hose, also known as braided vinyl tubing, to expand your space. This extension can also allow you to hide the timer and pressure reducer under a landscape valve box. Because the faucet will stay on continuously so that water will flow when the timer engages, you will need a Y valve at the hose outlet. This way, you can access the water for hand watering when you need it without having to turn the timed system on and off. Dismantle these connections in the late fall to avoid damage from freezing.

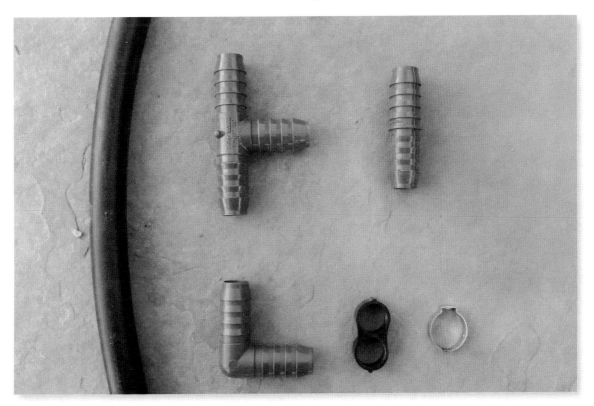

Photograph 6.3 Half inch parts - Poly tubing, T, connector, right angle, figure 8, and clamp.

Filter

In an irrigation system, water reaches each plant through a tiny opening from the main system. This hole can easily become plugged and prevent a plant from receiving proper watering. Filters installed with the timer and pressure reducer prevent clogging downstream. Clean out your filter every spring.

Photograph 6.4 Tools for half-inch line - hammer, clamp pliers, poly tube cutter, landscape staples.

Pressure reducer

Drip irrigation systems can't handle city water pressure (about 60 pounds per square inch, or PSI), and so these systems can easily blow out if this pressure isn't properly managed. Purchase a pressure reducer, which will reduce the pressure to 20 or 30 PSI. Screw the pressure reducer onto the bottom of the filter. Sometimes, you can find a combination filter and pressure reducer.

Helpful Notes: Parts and Tool List for Installing a Hose Bib Irrigation System

- Hose Y

- Metal washing machine hose, also knows as braided vinyl tubing (optional)

- Landscape box (optional)

- Timer

- Filter

- Pressure reducer

- Teflon tape for sealing connecting pieces

- Depending on what you purchase from the array of timers, filters and pressure reducers available, you may need connector pieces between parts. Put the system together with an employee at the irrigation store so you know you have all the necessary parts.

Different Ways to Emit Water

 ## Soaker Hoses

A hose bib system can hook up to a sequence of emitters or to a soaker hose. To use a soaker hose, attach a garden hose to your timer/filter/pressure reducer and run it to your garden. At the growing area, attach a soaker hose and run it down the middle of your growing area. A soaker hose waters six inches across, puts out lots of water quickly, and soaks a large area. The disadvantages of soaker hoses are that they are surprisingly expensive and have a notoriously short life span. They can also kink and wear easily. Extend their life by making sure they are always covered with mulch and not exposed to the sun.

The Drip System

Helpful Notes: List of Parts from Mainline to Drip
(This pertains to both hose bib and multiple-zone systems)

- ½"poly tubing
- ½" metal clamps
- Clamp wrench
- ½" T for splitting the main line
- ½" connectors for line repairs
- Cutter for plastic tubing
- Figure 8 for the end of the line
- Hole puncher
- 1/4 straight barred
- Spagetti tubing (⅓"poly tubing)
- ⅓" Ts
- Emmiters: they come sized for 1, 2, or 4 gallons of water per hour
- 6" or 12" spaced in-line
- Bubble emitters
- Goof plugs
- Landscape staples
- A hammer for stapling

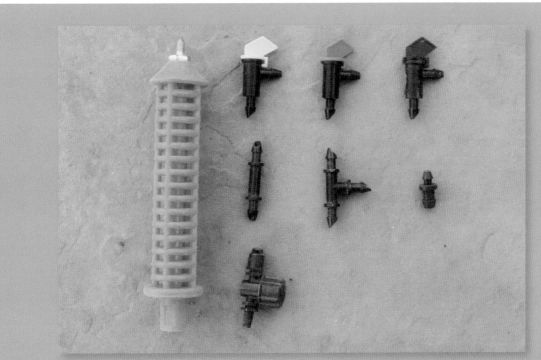

Photograph 6.5 Quarter inch parts - hole puncher, 3 different emitters, connector, T, goof plug, micro-sprayer.

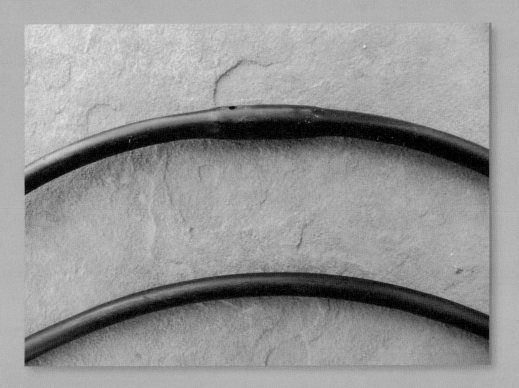

Photograph 6.6 Quarter inch in-line (on top) and Quarter inch spaghetti tubing.

⬤ Half-inch tubing

If you are creating an emitter system, half-inch poly tubing channels water from the hose source to the growing areas. In a multiple-line system, these will extend out from the valve box. It is the main water artery you will tap into to run emitters for a single plant or a drip line for an overall area.

The half-inch tubing attaches at the vacuum breaker in a multiple-zone system, and at the filter of a hose bib system. Seal the connection with a metal clamp. Run your line to your growing areas. Install a ½-inch T to split the line, securing every connection with metal clamps. Do not bury your line. You will need to find it often when planning plantings, before digging, or to tap into. Also, if you bury a line, roots will grow over it which then must be damaged if the line is ever moved again. Instead, lay the line on the ground before mulching. Staple down the tubing with 6-inch irrigation staples as needed. Staples prevent the line from shifting or getting pulled out from beneath the mulch. Mulch covers the unattractive tubing and is easy to move aside when you want to find the line.

Lay the line so that it is close to planting areas. Draw a sketch of where you laid the line and file your drawing with your landscape design. No matter how good your memory, at some point you will surely ask yourself "Where did I put that line?". An irrigation system map also helps future homeowners work with your system.

Some irrigation companies use ¾-inch irrigation tubing instead of ½-inch tubing. Use ¾-inch tubing when going long distances from faucet to garden. The smaller diameter is effective for most city lots on city water systems. We suggest ¾-inch tubing when pulling from a rainwater cistern.

Close off the end of your main line with a figure 8. A figure 8 allows you to slide the ½-inch tube through one hole, then pinch it back through the adjacent hole.

Spaghetti Tubing (1/3" Poly Tubing) and Emitters

Use emitters for watering an individual plant at its root ball. With a hole puncher, tap into the main line, the ½-inch tubing, nearest your plant. Insert a ¼"connector. Often, your hole puncher will have a gadget that will help you insert your connector into the main line. Be careful on hot days, when the ½ inch tubing is soft from the heat, that you do not stab the hole-puncher through both sides of the main line. Connect the appropriate length of spaghetti tubing to the connector. At the plant's root line, use a ¼-inch T to split the line. Place two more shorts strips of spaghetti tubing on each side of the T to make a ring around the plant. Finish with two 1- or 2-gallon emitters for perennials and two 4-gallon emitters for trees (depending on the species). Staple your line into the ground.

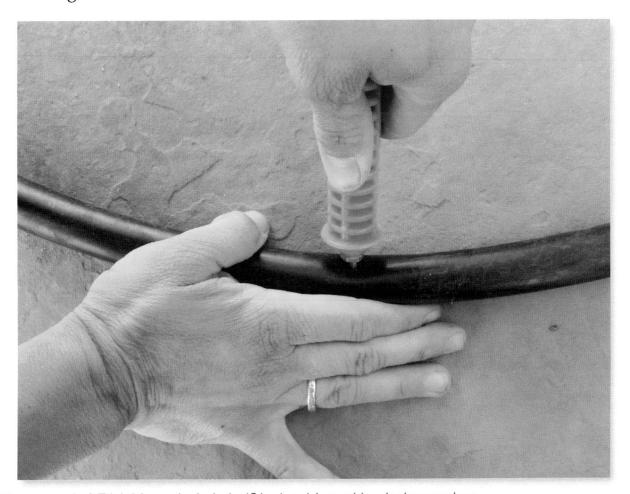

Photograph 6.7 Making a hole in half-inch tubing with a hole puncher.

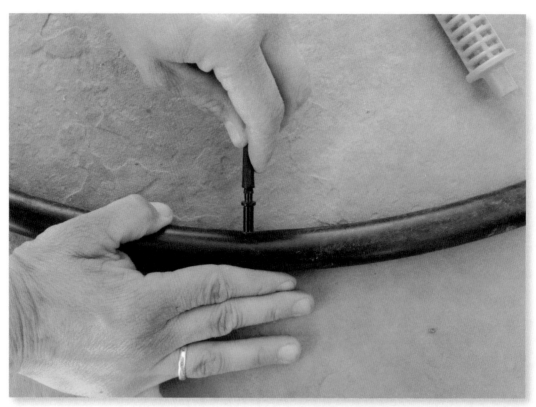

Photograph 6.8 Connecting spaghetti tubing to connector which connects to the main line.

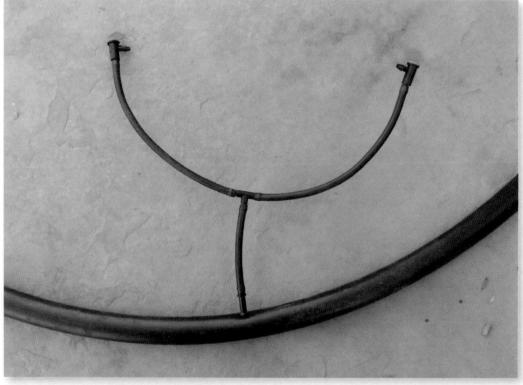

6.9 Emitter configuration from main line.

Emitter placement is important. Imagine the wet area beneath the soil after a watering. A plant's roots will stay where the water is. So if you have emitters right at the base of a plant, its roots will never grow out. As a result, the plant will stay rather small and fail to develop the strength it needs to expand.

A circumscribed root system keeps a plant more dependent on supplemental water because it is not able to draw water from a wider base. Instead, train your plant to grow wide, deep roots so that at some point, you can cease supplemental water in all but times of drought. You want half of that wet area to be above the existing roots so they don't have to work at all to establish themselves in this new environment. You want the second half of the wet area further out from the root ball to encourage the roots to expand. When you are planting a new plant, of course you can see how wide the root ball is, and place the emitter just beyond the reach of the root ball. If you are adding irrigation to an existing plant, remember that root balls tend to end at the plant's drip line, the vertical line from the outermost leaves to the ground below them. To make sure your root balls continue to expand year after year, widen the drip from the emitter or emitters during spring irrigation maintenance. On steep slopes, add water-catchment berms below irrigated plants to prevent run-off.

In-lines or Drip Lines Water Whole Areas

In-line looks just like spaghetti tubing but has holes every 6 or 12 inches. In-line connects to the main line, loops out to water the necessary area, and then reconnects to the main line.

Six-inch spaced drip lines are an effective way to water vegetable gardens. When installing, leave yourself some spare line so that you can easily adjust it. Each time you add a seedling, revise where your drip line is situated so that the base of the new plant receives water from a couple of holes in the tubing. With seeds, drip-line watering is an effective and sometimes life-saving supplement to hand watering. However, you will still need to check or hand water seeds once or twice a day.

Also, install an inline around trees to supplement emitters. To assure the tree develops a strong root system, run an undulating 6- or 12-inch spaced in-line at the tree's drip line. Create a closed loop by connecting both ends of inline into the mainline. After stapling the line down, it should look like the petals of a daisy. This method can help older, struggling trees come back to life.

6.10 In-Line Daisy Configuration Around A Tree.

 ## Bubbler Emitters

Bubbler emitters are very low-to-the-ground sprinklers, delivering water to targeted locations. They are less effective as water conservers than emitters, but are water-saving heroes compared to sprinklers. Bubbler emitters are good for densely-planted areas, such as vegetable seeds, native lawns, or tightly-planted flowerbeds. Connect them directly into the ½-inch line tubing.

When and How Much Should You Water?

Always water in the early mornings or the late evenings to reduce water loss due to evaporation. Evenings are ideal because the plants have all night to absorb the water before they must compete with the sun. All watering suggestions assume that proper drought-resistant varieties and species have been chosen for your garden area.

Watering Trees, Shrubs, and Perennials

To establish trees, water twice weekly, an hour a day, for the first few weeks. Then, gradually decrease to once weekly for 90 minutes, then every 10 days the first year. Under normal circumstances, well-adapted plants can be watered twice monthly in summer and monthly the rest of the year if the water soaks in 30 inches. If irrigation water pools and doesn't soak in, add sponges around the tree (see Chapter Seven). To establish shrubs and perennials, water twice weekly, 20 to 30 minutes a day. Water more frequently in the hot days of summer. Native trees and shrubs take a couple of years to get well established. Fruit trees and novelty species may take at least three years to get established.

After shrubs and perennials are established, cut back to a single weekly watering. In this book, we encourage people to plant lots of food-producing trees and shrubs. These are relatively high water users compared to dryland native and adapted species, which would only need watering every couple of weeks after establishment. We justify the extra water use for growing food by also encouraging rainwater harvesting. Wherever your food is grown, water is used. Then food has to travel to your plate. To produce one gallon of gas requires five gallons of water. So if you want to protect our fresh water supply, grow your food within walking distance.

Eliminate supplemental water when the local rainy season begins, and during the winter when a plant's water needs are minimal. With a proper passive rainwater harvesting system in place, plants can survive and actually become stronger during the fall and winter without supplemental watering if they get a bit of snow or rain. During dry winters, plants and trees need monthly deep watering. Do this on warm days when the ground is not frozen. Plants grow roots during the winter and still need moisture.

Begin watering again in the early spring. Care for your plants but make them push themselves a bit to survive. This will help them become hardy and resilient.

Pay attention to your plants and notice any signs of stress. Wilted or curled leaves or leaf drop indicate a lack of water. Expect some plants, especially broad-leafed veggies, to wilt mid-day in the southwestern climate. Even in saturated soil, plants cannot take up as much water as evaporates through their leaves during hot summer days. Observe them at sunset. If they haven't bounced back by then, check emitters to make sure they are working properly and give plants a refreshing drink to help them along.

Watering in Vegetable and Flower Gardens

Annual gardens need closer monitoring than perennial growth, but you can still automate the watering system. Vegetable seeds, and seedlings especially, need daily or even twice daily watering, depending on whether or not they are covered with row-cover (discussed in detail in Chapter Nine). If you rely only on hand watering, young plants can tie you to your land. Irrigating your veggies offers you more freedom to be gone from home, although it is always important to have someone checking to make sure the system is working during the heat of the summer.

As plants mature and root systems develop, encourage your veggies to "get tough" by extending the periods between watering. At full growth, water once or twice a week. Some plants such as peppers and tomatoes like less water when producing fruit. Overwatering plants like these produces waxy fruit, which is lower in sugar, and therefore lower in taste and nutritional value. Choose drought-tolerant heirloom species and use 2 to 3 inches of mulch (straw, leaves, or grass clippings) to double the benefit of the water you use. We like to purchase heirloom, native seeds from nativeseeds.org. You can also purchase heirloom seeds from Baker Creek Heirloom Seeds, rareseeds.com and D. Landreth Seed Company, landrethseeds.com.

The disadvantage of timer-irrigated veggies is that often they are not observed as closely. Hand watering creates wonderful opportunities to monitor plant health, watch for early signs of pests and disease, and witness flowering and fruiting. If you use an automated system, take frequent strolls around your garden to notice what's happening with your plants.

Irrigation System Maintenance

Spring seems a natural season to do a maintenance check on your entire irrigation system. Run the system on manual for 30 minutes. After the system turns on, walk your line and look for and listen for leaks. Visit each irrigated plant. Find the emitters for each plant and make sure they are flowing. The most common problem in an irrigation system is clogged emitters. Because of this, install flag emitters, which are easy to clean out.

On a flag emitter, a flag on the backside of the emitter unscrews and lets out a stream of high-pressure water, flushing any debris that might otherwise clog the drip. Beware not to squirt yourself in the face as you studiously examine your emitter!

To clean out the filter, unscrew it and rinse it out under water.

In-lines will typically need repositioning in annual veggie gardens to make sure all plants from this year's season are covered.

Irrigation maintenance may intimidate some, especially for the right-brain thinkers who are put off by the word "system." But every visit to your garden can be fun. While you are spending time with your plants during irrigation maintenance, try talking to each of them. Ask it how it likes its spot and its neighbor plants. Is it getting all its needs met? When we care for our families by giving them food and water, we don't just throw it down in front of them and leave. We sit down with them, talk about our day, comment about the food and drink. Treat your garden maintenance the same way. If you do this, maintenance will stop feeling like a chore and start feeling like meditation and bonding with your plants.

Our Home Farms
From Melanie

When we were writing this book, my home farm was in the early stages of evolutionary development. The first summer I watered everything by hand. I spent hours watering every week, and my water bills were way too high! However, I felt very intimately connected with each and every plant in the garden. The second summer, I installed a hose bib system with soaker hoses. This helped me to a large extent, because I could turn on part of the watering system and let the watering happen as I did other things in the morning, like getting ready for work. However, the watering was not as precise as it was the previous summer, and I did not have as close a daily relationship with all of my plants. I learned that regardless of what kind of system I was using, it was still very important for me to get all the way out into my garden, and connect with each plant every day, even if briefly.

From Zoe

We have two hose bib drip systems. One extends to our vegetable beds from the rainwater cistern and the other sources city water and extends to our food forest. We tend to hand water with rainwater in the spring as plants pop up here and there and wonder is everywhere in the garden. Sometime every year about the end of May or first part of June, watering gets less and less fun and I "forget" to do it more and more. That's why we've taken to tweaking our irrigation system every May so when that watering-is-a-chore season hits, we are ready to switch over to an automatic system. We established our food forest line when we first planted it several years ago. Bard waters the food forest once a week in the summer months, then turns the system off when the monsoons come. As much as we try to avoid using city water, having a city water fallback plan is really vital when it comes to plant establishment and times of drought. Each year, we try to extend our time off the system before we turn it back on in the spring. Drylands landscaping expert Judith Phillips advocates that we should let plants come into blossom on their own accord, without pushing them into budding with early spring irrigating. As climate change continues to increase out-of-season storms, like a late freeze or a mid-winter warm-up that triggers all the plants to bolt too early, it is best to let plants sleep by not giving them water until they wake up on their own.

 Exercise 6.1

This chapter has provided a lot of information about irrigation systems, and for some people all this information may seem daunting. Take a few minutes to think about where you are with respect to your plans for a watering system by answering the following questions:

1. What is the location/locations of the hose bib, or hose bibs, in your garden? How are these situated in relationship to your trees, shrubs, perennials, and annual gardens of vegetables and flowers?

2. Do you have an irrigation system installed at your home? If so, do you know where the main control box is located? And do you know how to use your timer, and/or have an instruction manual for it?

3. What kind of irrigation system or systems do you want to implement in your garden in the next growing season?:
   - hand watering
   - hose bib system with drip hoses, operated manually
   - hose bib system with drip hoses, operated from a timer
   - drip irrigation system with an automatic timer

4. Will you do the installation work on your irrigation system yourself? Will you need help? If so, who can you find to help you make the

project approachable and fun? Or will you hire someone to do this work for you? If so, do you have a vendor already, or know someone who can recommend a good vendor for you?

5. Make a quick sketch of whatever you already know about what type of watering system you plan to implement in your garden this summer, and what you will locate where.

Congratulations! Just by thinking about these questions you are well on your way to keeping your plants happy, fat, and sassy.

Your Notes

section 3

Plant Life

This section will teach you how to choose and cultivate plants for food, medicine, beauty, and support of other desirable creatures in your home farm ecosystem.

Along the way you will learn how to plant fruit trees and food forests. You will also learn how to plan, plant, and nourish successful vegetable gardens. You will receive tips and tricks for seed saving and pest control.

Chapter Seven:

Food Forests

Overview

A food forest is a low input, long-term output way of growing food. Traditional farms often include all the aspects of a food forest with separate areas for orchards, vegetable production, and herb beds. In a food forest, these crops are all raised in one area. Instead of spreading food production out over large acreage, homeowners maximize production from small spaces by growing in vertical layers. In food forests, farmers do not work towards maximum yield from a single plant, but rather towards a combined, diverse output. Like all other aspects of our home farms, a food forest is a work in progress and will be implemented differently in each unique location to meet each homeowner's particular needs.

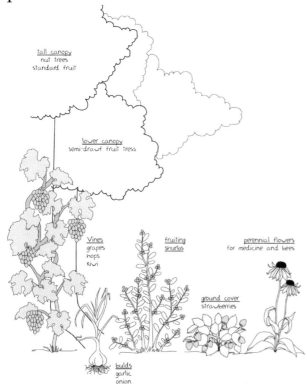

A food forest includes four layers of growth:

1. The upper canopy of trees-nuts, standard fruit, and cottonwoods;

2. The lower canopy of semi-dwarf and dwarf fruit trees and nitrogen fixers, and shrubs (berry producing or nitrogen fixing);

3. Perennial herbs, vegetables and ground cover; and

4. Vines and roots.

Drawing 7.1 Layers of a Food Forest

In this chapter, we will explore how food forests work and their benefits. We will discuss each layer of the food forest, giving extra attention to the canopy, and examining how to plant and maintain a fruit tree properly. Finally, we will give a brief description of a fruit tree guild, cousin to the food forest.

Photograph 7.1 A Developing Food Forest

Why Incorporate a Food Forest into Your Home Farm?

 Low Human Input

A standard practice for food forests is that the soil is rarely dug after the initial planting, and all the foods included are perennials so they will produce year after year. If annuals are incorporated, self-seeding species are selected. Seasonal pruning and irrigation maintenance is the only human input needed. Because of this, if you want to lower your carbon footprint by growing your own food, but aren't interested in tinkering regularly in a vegetable garden, you may wish to convert the majority of your yard into a food forest.

Low Resource Input

If appropriate species are chosen for your ecosystem, perennial growth requires fewer nutrients and less water than annual growth. When installed correctly, with passive rainwater harvesting techniques and greywater, an irrigation system, and a thick layer of mulch, perennial growth takes relatively little water. This chapter will discuss species you can incorporate into your food forest for natural soil fertilization. Otherwise, a food forest will thrive with only an occasional application of compost tea (see Chapter Nine for how to make compost tea). With low resource requirements and proximity to the home, food forests may be the most sustainable, earth-friendly way to grow food.

 ## Makes Each Garden Feature Perform Multiple Functions

Because food forests produce thick layers of growth, they make beautiful and useful green fences, blocking wind and noise as well as hiding unattractive man-made fences and walls. Since they require low maintenance, they can be planted far from the house.

 ## A Multi-generational Investment

Food forests are not a new idea. Agriculturist Geoff Lawton discovered a 300-year-old, two-acre food forest in Vietnam. The family that lives there told him they are the 28th generation to use and tend the food forest. In this two-acre food forest, every plant and tree has a story and a purpose. The family uses the forest constantly, every meal has ingredients from their yard, and all their medicine is produced right there. Through this example, we recognize the return-on-investment potential of food forests.

How Food Forests Work

 **Succession**

If water is available, bare land will become a forest. In arid climates, this is limited to areas with shallow groundwater and/or periodic surface flooding. Forests have the greatest life capacity of any ecosystem and nature is always attempting to create more life. The semi-predictable evolution of bare land to forest is called succession. In nature, finding bare dirt is rare. The moment dirt is exposed, succession begins. Only with the invention of agriculture and with human development do we find great expanses of bare dirt.

The pioneering species of plants arrive on the scene first, including aggressive weeds and grasses. Pioneer species thrive by finding water quickly. They seem to grow from nothing, like Russian thistle, also known as tumbleweed. Pioneer plants hold soil in place, catch debris that travel over the area, and create mulch with their own plant material. If you want a new perspective on an unpopular weed like tumbleweed, look at one growing in a bare field and notice the organic matter collected around its base. Put your finger in the soil and see if it isn't more moist there than the bare ground three feet away. You can see that tumbleweeds, although perhaps annoying, are serving a purpose by laying a foundation for more desirable species to take hold.

The next type of species to appear in the evolution of a forest is scrubs. These are low-growing shrubs and briars. Before trees develop, swaths of shrubs seem to grow on and entangle an area.

Next, pioneering trees like honey locusts sprout up. These trees are short-lived but break up the ground and provide thick mulch layers that build soil.

Slowly, longer-lived trees develop, like cottonwoods and oaks. As these large canopy trees shade the understory, shrubs compete for light. What once was a great area of wild roses, for example, now becomes a place with a few hearty, well-located plants. Much of the understory then waits for trees to fall to create a break in the canopy, and the opportunity to receive direct sunlight.

In the desert, this process is limited by water. However, given time, even deserts develop taller and taller species of plants with companion understories, like a Saguaro cactus with yuccas tucked beneath it. The Sonoran Desert supports the growth of arid-adapted trees such as ironwood, palo verde and acacia. The Chihuahuan Desert is primarily a shrub desert or desert grassland.[1]

Unsightly and aggressive weeds agitate most urban dwellers who don't understand their role in the larger process of creating abundance. Most homeowners respond by eradicating the weeds one way or another, bagging them, and removing them from the site. If the land remains bare, this keeps it constantly at that first step of succession and will forever ensure more weed growth.

If we understand the process of succession, we know that weeds are only making mulch for more valuable species. We can facilitate the natural process by mulching heavily and accelerate the evolution toward having a weed-free space. In a food forest, we speed up the natural process a whole generation by planting multiple layers of food-producing species.

Filling a Niche

Different layers of the food forest thrive together because they find their niche in space and time with respect to each other. The saying goes, "as above, so below" – different layers of above ground growth mirror different layers of root systems. A strawberry plant roots in the top few inches of soil. A yarrow plant collects water in the soil below that and an apple tree uses water even deeper below the soil surface. So, the three can peacefully co-exist near each other without competing for water.

The layers of a food forest also represent niches in time. The forest leafs out from the bottom up. Lower-growing plants, such as garlic, chives, dandelion, and sorrel, thrive in spring when the most light is available. Top layers leaf late to avoid frost. The entire food forest production peaks in spring, before annual production peaks, making a great companion for annual garden space.

---

[1] Judith Phillips

Keeping and Using Every Bit of Water Available

Bare soil sheds rainwater quickly, sometimes immediately. Compacted, bare soil returns to dust alarmingly fast after a rain because not much water is absorbed and it then evaporates quickly. In a food forest, hard rains hit the leaves of trees. Raindrops splinter and drip down onto the shrub story, slowing the water again. The slower water travels, the more time it has to absorb into the soil. By the time hard rains reach the soil of a forest floor, the velocity of the water has slowed considerably. Mulch created by the forest absorbs water like a sponge. Shallow root systems act like straws pulling water into the ground immediately. Because water attracts water, once the soil is wet, it can absorb more water. Lower root systems pull the water deeper and deeper into the soil. Once the rains stop and the clouds clear, the sun begins immediately to evaporate groundwater. In a food forest, however, the ground has a canopy of shade from all the different layers of growth to slow down the evaporation process. Underground, there are layers of roots holding onto the water around them, further reducing evaporation.

The Canopy of Your Food Forest

The top and middle canopy of the food forest is mostly fruiting trees. In large areas, one can divide this category into a higher canopy of nut and standard fruit trees, and a lower canopy of dwarf or semi-dwarf fruit trees. In many urban yards, the space needed for a standard-sized fruit tree would limit the number of trees the area can handle. Dwarf trees are not fierce competitors so they do not produce well in the shade of a standard-sized fruit tree. Using semi-dwarf fruit trees as the top layer allows for more diversity since you can fit more of them into a space successfully. They also fruit several years before standards, and are easy to reach for pruning and harvesting. If space allows for a high canopy tree, walnuts, almonds, and pecans make good backdrop choices and can provide you with excellent sources of protein and healthy fat.

In some climates, light is a limiting factor for food forest production. Fortunately, in the arid Southwest, the light is so intense that this is rarely an issue. Instead, we are limited by soil fertility and water. To address these issues, mulch heavily and continue to mulch every couple of years so the soil always has rich nutrients. Secondly, make sure that you utilize the passive rainwater harvesting techniques suggested earlier in this book to maximize your use of rainwater and flush salt out of your soil.

To determine how many trees can fit into your food forest, estimate the mature size of each type of tree. Trees tend to stay small in desert soil due to low soil fertility and limited rainwater. Here are a few suggestions for the types of fruiting trees you may want to consider choosing:

- Cherry (shrub and tree)
- Pears, plums, and peach trees
- Apple and quince
- Figs
- Apricot
- Mulberry, black and white

Fast-Growing-Trees.com has a nice section on their website which lists trees for each state.

Helpful Notes: How to Plant a Fruit Tree

In other parts of the country, it is recommended to dig a hole twice as wide and deep as the root ball and amend the soil with compost. However, this is not the best practice in the desert Southwest. Roots seek out nutrients. Because our soil is naturally nutrient-poor, if the area around the root ball is the richest available because it has been amended, roots will stay in that small area. This will restrict the growth of the tree above and below ground and will make it more susceptible to perishing during times of drought.

Instead, dig a hole no deeper than the depth of the pot and only slightly wider than the width of the roots. Loosen the roots of the tree. I call this tickling its toes because I imagine it must feel exhilarating for root-bound plants to stretch out. If roots have started to grow in a circle around the pot, they will continue in that motion even in the ground. So give the roots a good loosening even if it means breaking some. Use a soil knife if necessary. Drop the tree into the hole and fill the hole with dirt.

Do not plant too deep. Keep the base of the trunk at the same level it was in the pot. A tree planted too deep will be stressed.

Then, dig up to three *sponges* (described in detail in Chapter Three) 6 to 12 inches beyond the border of the original hole. Keep these sponges wet during the first season after planting. The tree will sense the nearby water source, forcing it to extend its roots outward and establish itself quickly. Irrigate according to directions in Chapter Six.

Finally, top-dress the area around the tree with compost and mulch, keeping it away from the base of the tree. This way, nutrients will seep into the ground slowly and improve the soil all around the tree.

Groworganic.com is another source for fruit trees, as is treesofantiquity.com which sells heirloom fruit trees.

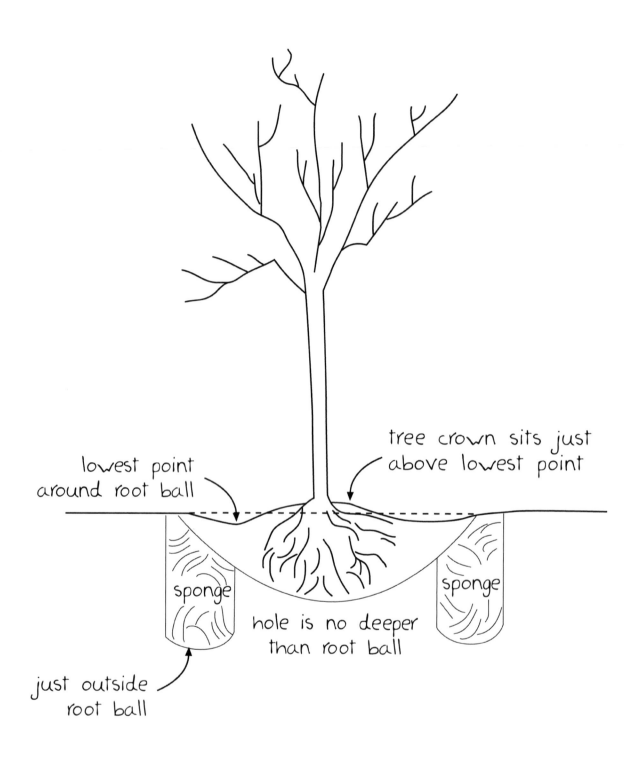

Drawing 7.2 How to Plant a Fruit Tree.

Pruning Influences the Shape and Size of a Tree

Unpruned trees tend to look more like bushes with short trunks and lots of branches. Unpruned trees have an overall higher yield of fruit than pruned trees, but with much smaller pieces of fruit that tend to grow at the ends of the branches. Pruned trees produce larger pieces of fruit, which are more marketable if you intend to sell your surplus. Also, unpruned trees ususally produce fruit only every other year, compared to the more regular crop of the pruned tree.

February is the best month to prune, but any time when the tree is dormant is fine. Avoid pruning after leaves have formed. Do not prune in extreme cold.

Prune lower branches in order to encourage the tree to have a taller canopy. Thin out straggly branches and branch clusters as well as the "suckers" that pop up around the tree base. This will keep energy consolidated into strong, choice branches. If a tree starts to split into a Y, cut the weaker of the two branches early. A Y in a fruit tree is structurally weak, and makes the tree prone to splitting during storms or under the weight of heavy fruit. If both sides of the Y are well developed, choose the smaller to become a subordinate branch by cutting it 12 inches above the split.

 # Espaliers

A fruit tree that has been trained and pruned to grow horizontally along wires is called an espalier. This is most commonly done with apple and pear trees. Espaliers can help to maximize growing space and cool heat-absorbing walls. Placing the espalier against a south-facing wall utilizes warmer micro-climates for some fruit tree varieties, like figs, that prefer warmer growth conditions. Growing against north-facing walls can prevent premature budding for fruit trees that are not cold-hardy or early-blooming fruit trees, such as apricot and plum. A north wall keeps them colder for longer into the spring, delaying their blooming and promising a more frequent fruit crop.

Photograph 7.2 Fruit Tree Being Trained to Grow on an Espalier - Courtesy of Carol Bennett

Other Food Forest Layers

 ## Understory - Shrub Layer

Commonly known as soft fruits, this shrub layer can be subdivided into bush fruits (currants, gooseberries, sand cherries) and cane fruits (raspberries, blackberries). Bush fruits are not drought-tolerant, but the examples given here require relatively little water. Raspberries and blackberries have high water needs and grow best around greywater outlets. Flowering and fruiting depend on access to light, so shrubs may produce best in the years while trees are establishing themselves.

Place shrubs where you expect the drip line to be for mature, neighboring fruit trees. This will maximize the moisture available to each plant and ensure that the shrubs will get plenty of light.

Examples of drought-tolerant shrubs are native roses, Nanking cherries, native plums, three-leaf sumac, winterfat, Apache plume, fernbush, chamisa, cliffrose, and cinquefoil.

 ## Ground Level - Perennial Fruits, Vegetables, Herbs, and Flowers

In the spaces between the other plants in your food forest, perennials provide opportunities for food and medicine, beauty, and bee-forage. The possibilities for this category are enormous. Perennial fruit/vegetable options include rhubarb, artichoke, Egyptian onion, walking onion, chives, strawberry, sorrel, salad burnet, and asparagus. You can select what varieties you want to plant according to local availability and your personal preference. Perennial herbs for cooking and medicine include rosemary, thyme, all varieties of sages, stinging nettles, garlic chives, lovage, mullein, valerian, Echinacea, lavender, yarrow, anise, and mint. Plant the most sun-loving species, such as rosemary, thyme and asparagus, on the outside edges of the bed.

Drought-resistant flowers are a welcome addition to the lower level of a food forest. Take time to study what flowers also serve as medicine in order to stack functions most effectively in your garden. Even if flowers are not medicinal, however, they still provide beauty and bee forage, and attract other pollinators.

 ## The Climbing Layer – Vines

Where scarce light limits growth, including vines in a food forest can create too much competition, but this is not usually a limiting factor in the Southwest. Vines can grow up established trees, along fences, against walls with attached wire supports, and up the posts of shade structures. They cool hot adobe walls and add shade to sitting areas. Grapes grow well in sandy, low-nutrient soils and several drought-tolerant varieties are available. Bunches of grapes hanging from an arbor symbolize abundance and beckon visitors. Other vines that grow well in arid climates are kiwis (these require male and female plants to be located near each other) as well as hops for making beer.

Photograph 7.3 Grape Vines Growing on Zoe and Bard's Shade Structure

 # Specialty Plants

Nitrogen Fixers

Some plants, called *nitrogen fixers*, have a symbiotic relationship with soil bacteria that gather nitrogen from the air. Nitrogen fixers capture the nitrogen from this bacteria and store it in their leaves and nodules at the end of root branches. Because nitrogen is the single most important chemical to promote plant production, incorporating nitrogen fixers in your food forest will greatly improve its productivity. Siberian pea shrub, false indigo bush, Apache plume, velvet mesquite, sea buckthorn, and alfalfa all fix nitrogen and are great additions to a self-fertilizing food forest.

To make nitrogen available to neighboring plants, trim the leaves of nitrogen fixers and lay these leaves directly on the ground around fruiting trees. As the leaves break down, they will release readily available nitrogen into the soil for whatever is growing there. Secondly, because of the law of "as above, so below," roots that mirror trimmed branches will die back and their nodules will release nitrogen into the soil.

Dynamic Accumulators

While nitrogen fixers collect nutrients from the air, dynamic accumulators mine nutrients from the soil. Soils may contain enough nutrients, apart from nitrogen, to grow all the fruits and vegetables we might plant in our back yards. Yet these nutrients are often in a form that is relatively unavailable to plants.

Dynamic accumulators have special adaptive skills to extract these specific nutrients. When these plants or their leaves die, they make these nutrients accessible to neighboring plants. Different plants mine different nutrients. For example comfrey excels at mining potassium, while legumes harvest phosphorous. If you identify some of these plants in your yard, note that they are serving an important role beneath the soil surface.

Photograph 7.4 Comfrey Planted Near a Fig Tree

Helpful Notes:

Examples of Dynamic Accumulators

- comfrey
- dandelion
- meadow sweet
- lamb's quarters
- garlic
- yarrow
- fennel
- watercress
- purslane
- buckwheat
- parsley
- wild strawberry
- peppermint
- chamomile
- stinging nettle
- thistle
- vetch
- plantain
- bind weed (can you believe it?!)

Roots & Bulbs

Some food foresters include root crops as the final layer of the food forest. Jerusalem artichoke is a good example of a wild, edible root. It seems to do better in the Southwest, where it doesn't have enough water to overtake an area as it can in wetter climates. I like to add spring flower bulbs in moist areas of a food forest. Judith Phillips, the drylands landscaping expert who gave us input for this book, claims that tulip flowers make great salad cups and the petals taste like green pea! Their beauty lightens the heart after a long, drab winter, and they require only minimum watering.

Fruit Tree Guild

A fruit tree guild is a miniature version of the food forest. A guild is organized around a single fruit tree, structuring the bed. Beneath the tree layer are small shrubs and perennials. Farther away from the fruit tree than the perennials, you can grow annuals. At Mother Nature Gardens, several of our vegetable beds are fruit tree guilds. These have all the same benefits of added water conservation and absorption as in the food forest. A properly-planted fruit tree guild is very successful at deterring insects from both the fruit tree and the vegetables planted in the guild.

Photograph 7.5 Fruit Tree Guild

Helpful Notes:

Examples of Plants for an Apple Guild
(sourced from sunstoneherbs.com):

- Apple tree
- Comfrey
- Rhubarb
- Dill
- Cilantro
- Yarrow
- Walking onions
- Lemon balm
- Dandelions
- Chicory
- Grapes
- Currants
- Lavender
- Alfalfa
- Thyme
- Siberian pea shrub
- Garden sage

Exercise 7.1 Your Food Forest

Take a few minutes to consider where and how you might establish a food forest as part of your home farm:

1. Where on your property would you locate your food forest?

2. What will be the watering source/sources for your food forest?

3. What fruit, nut, and other types of trees do you want to include in the upper canopy of your food forest?

4. What semi-dwarf and dwarf fruit trees and nitrogen fixers do you want to include in the lower canopy of your food forest?

5. What berry-producing or nitrogen-fixing shrubs do you want to include in the shrub layer of your food forest?

6. What perennial herbs and vegetables will you grow under the shrub layer?

7. What will you include as ground cover?

8. Will you include vines in your food forest, that grow up from the ground to the higher layers?

9. What root crops would you like to grow under the ground?

Chapter Eight:

Preparing the Vegetable Garden

Overview

Much of the work of growing vegetables takes place long before the seeds go into the ground. New gardeners often don't start thinking about their gardens early enough in the year. To get a good sense of garden timing, think in terms of seasons:

- Build soil in the *fall.*

- Plan your garden (shop seed catalogs, get your starts ready, etc.) in the *winter.*

- Plant in the *spring.* (Chapter Nine discusses extended season gardening.)

- Maintain and harvest in the *summer.*

So, in order to get an abundant crop of veggies in mid-August, ideally prepare for those tomatoes, squash, and peppers nine months earlier!   No wonder it takes people a few years to get into the rhythm of gardening.

In this chapter, you'll learn about the community style of gardening, versus growing veggies in rows. This approach will help shape your beds before you prepare the soil. Although these techniques may be strange for a person with traditional gardening experience, they produce high yield in small spaces with low input. Next, you will gain insight into one of the most important aspects of farming: growing soil. You will learn seasonal methods to build great soil, as well as quick ways to boost the health of your soil. Finally, you will have an opportunity to consider the powerful impact the moon has on your garden, and guidelines to begin aligning your gardening tasks with this lunar influence.

Community Methods of Gardening

 ## Planting in Beds vs. Rows

Every time we step on the soil around neat rows of veggies, the soil compacts, stressing existing roots and making the environment inhospitable to expanding roots. Instead, pull your rows together into a 3- to 4-foot bed where you can reach everything within from the pathway, creating definite edges between human territory and plant territory. This way, you increase growing space and the soil around your plants stays loose and aerated.

If an area of the bed is hard to reach, place a stepping stone there. This makes a permanent place to step, expands your reach, and creates one single point of compaction instead of many. Free from compaction, soil becomes more and more sponge-like every year, facilitating water absorption and root expansion.

Of course, planting beds need not have four sharp corners. If you are using rocks for borders, you can make the beds any shape you want. For example, we made our largest veggie bed at Mother Nature Gardens into an S curve for maximum edge effect. (Recall that we discussed the edge effect in Chapter Three as being a law of nature that asserts the interface, or edge, between two ecosystems creates a third, more complex system that combines elements of both. The edge offers a higher biodiversity than either of the two areas that meet to create it. In nature, this interface receives more light and nutrients and so is more productive.)

Photograph 8.1 Planting in Beds vs. in Row

Keyhole Gardens

One common way to maximize planting space is to create a keyhole garden. To make one, imagine taking a rectangular, 3- to 4-foot wide growing bed and curling it into a ring. Stop curling just before the end meets so you can walk into the circular center. The pathway is now only the 3- to 4-foot long entrance (as wide as you wish) and the inner circle surrounded by bed, giving the path a keyhole shape. These beds maximize growing space and are pleasing to the eye. (See Drawing 8.1 Keyhole Gardens.)

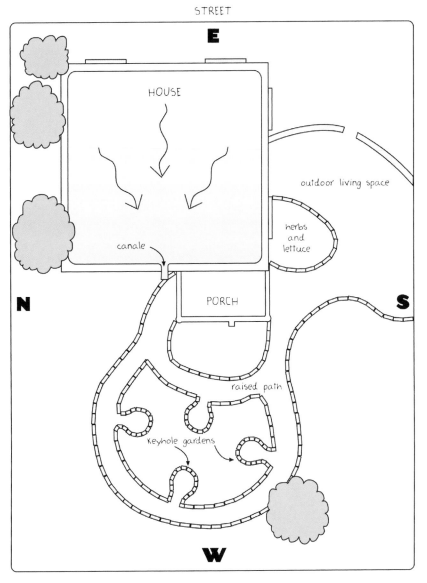

Drawing 8.1 Keyhole Gardens

Plant in Diverse Communities Modeled on a Food Forest

Maximize your growing space by filling your garden beds with diverse plants. Plants benefit from coming into contact with other types of plants. In a diverse garden bed, insects have to work harder to find a favorite crop. An aphid doesn't move from one cabbage to the next easily if a carrot and radish stand between them. Reasonable competition for water and nutrients creates stronger, more pest-resistant plants.

Treat your annual garden like a miniature food forest by blending your vegetable crops into diverse communities. Just like in a food forest, aim to maximize the overall production versus trying to maximize the yield of a single crop. A certain crop may do better in some years than in others. Yet, there will always be plenty of food to eat. Diversity increases food security because every year is different. One year, peppers may grow best while squash is a flop, while the next year, the opposite happens. You can learn why one year was better for a particular species by looking at weather, soil, rainfall, and other changing factors.

Also, model your annual garden on the layers described in a food forest. Sunflowers, corn, and sorghum, for example, provide a top canopy to shade tender plants below, and serve as poles for climbing beans and tomato supports. A huge range of shrubby vegetables can be used to fill the middle space. Make this layer more diverse by including some perennial flowering herbs and flowers to confuse hungry pests, and attract beneficial insects and pollinators. Colorful flowers make vegetable beds striking and fragrant (edible nasturtiums and marigolds are particular favorites), and perennial roots act to stabilize soil conditions for the annuals around them. Shade-loving plants, like lettuces and spinach, stay close to the ground. At Mother Nature Gardens, we have found that we can extend the growing season of spring veggies like lettuce and spinach, by planting them in the shade of taller plants like sunflowers and mullein. Root crops add a bottom layer in the veggie forest.

Many studies have been done about which plants prefer to grow with which other plants. In some circumstances, this information can be useful. At

Mother Nature Gardens, however, we don't plan these juxtapositions quite so rigorously. Because we have plant volunteers each year and veggies that have perennialized in our beds, we tend to have a disorderly hodge-podge of veggies and that seems to work for us.

Photograph 8.2 Planting Annuals in Diverse Communities

 **Our Home Farms**
From Zoe

At Mother Nature Gardens, when we first notice the days lengthening after the beginning of the year, we plant our cool season beds. Hoping for a diverse outcome and keeping things simple to save us time, we take our many seed packets of leafy greens and delicious root crops and mix them all together. We pull back the organic matter on the top of the beds and broadcast the mixed seeds. Then we cover with row cover. The seeds sprout like a ready mixed salad. When it is time to harvest a salad, we simply cut a section down. The next day, we cut the adjacent section and continue this pattern. By the time we get back to the first section, it has grown back.

Importance of Mulch

The forest produces mulch naturally when growth from past seasons accumulates on the ground. Microorganisms feed on the leaf debris, digesting it to create a rich soil that can sustain a diversity of plant life. This is an effective and sustainable growing method – recycling old life to feed new life.

Imitate this method by covering garden bed soil with a layer of straw two to three inches thick. Many materials make good mulch: straw, leaves, wood chips, pecan shells, sawdust, and newspaper all work to varying degrees. As the straw begins to break down, add a new layer. Fresh straw gives gardens a clean, bright look. If you add manure to the beds in the fall, this will counter any carbon buildup you might have from the breakdown of the straw. Remember from our compost section, soil building comes from equal parts green materials (high nitrogen materials like compost and green leaves) and brown materials (high carbon materials like mulch, straw, and paper products). If there is an imbalance of nitrogen materials and carbon materials, the resulting compost is poor. Carbon materials require nitrogen from green materials in order to break down. So an excess of carbon materials will rob the soil of nitrogen, and/or create carbon buildup in the soil. If the straw is on top of the soil, it will not rob nitrogen from the soil as much as if the straw is mixed into the soil.

To avoid rotting plant stems and insects munching seedlings and new transplants, leave a little space around the base of each plant. In our very dry New Mexican climate, we have successfully grown vegetables from seeds without clearing mulch from the dirt. However, keeping seedbeds and new transplants clear of mulch will help reduce stem rot.

In addition to feeding the soil, mulch insulates it, which lowers evaporation and keeps it cool. You will notice a significant drop in watering needs after covering bare dirt. Keep drip tubes beneath the mulch layer to further reduce evaporation.

Building Soil

Good soil makes the difference between a yellow, straggly-branched tomato plant and a tomato plant that pumps out a dozen tomato sauce dinners for you. In soil production, microorganisms do all the dirty work. A microorganism is any living organism too small to be seen with the naked eye. There are literally millions of them per handful of rich loam soil. They break down organic material (last year's leaf debris and your added mulch), liberating nutrients for use by plants. They need only organic material and moisture to do their work. So to build good soil, a farmer must provide plenty of food and ideal growing conditions for these organisms, either in a compost bin or in your garden beds.

In Chapter One we talked about evaluating the soil in your garden by conducting a simple soil composition test with a jar and water to determine soil structure. We also talked about pH and nutrient testing. Whatever the results of these tests, the remedy for correcting all imbalances includes adding organic matter, vermiculture-compost, or compost. (We'll discuss vermiculture in the section below.) Add compost and organic matter regularly to any neglected soil and it will heal and thrive in a few years.

Photograph 8.3 Good Soil

Most of us can't be sure of the history of our property or what pollutants might have contaminated our soils. If soil toxicity concerns you, contact the county extension agent to test for any major pollutants in the soil. If you want to address the possibility of having a lot of pollutants in your soil, spend the first season growing sunflowers, asters, and pennycress. These plants are known to clean heavy metals and toxins from soils. The following year, plant edibles in your newly cleaned soil.

Worm Boxes

A drawback of composting in arid lands is that compost piles need to be consistently moist to work effectively. That's why red worm bins are a brilliant choice for dry climates. Red worms must also stay moist but you keep them covered in a hole in the ground, so retaining moisture is easier to do than with a compost bin. Red worms are grown, bagged, and sold because of their voracious appetites for consuming coffee grounds and kitchen scraps. Their special brand of poop is call vermi-compost and is potent and nutrient-rich. Look for them at gardening stores or order them online.

Preparing a simple red worm home can take less than 15 minutes. To do so:

1. Dig a hole 3' x 3' x 6", a bit away from the house (it will attract other critters hoping to thrive) and in a relatively cool spot.

2. Drop in your bag of red worms.

3. Lay down a day or two of collected kitchen scraps or horse manure.

4. Cover with straw or shredded paper to keep your worms insulated and moisten.

5. Cover the hole with a lid. This can vary from an appropriately-sized piece of plywood to a well-constructed worm "door." To dump kitchens scraps, lift the lid, pull back the insulation, and feed your worms.

6. The only other care they need is to be kept moist. If you have the hose out to water your garden, don't forget to give your worms a shot of water too.

Bard creates a deluxe version of this concept for some customers – bottomless wooden boxes that he submerges up to the lid in the ground. All the other details remain the same, but the aesthetics are more pleasing.

In three to four months, depending on how much you feed your worms, you will have a harvest of vermi-compost, also called castings, ready at the bottom of your worm bin. Compared to ordinary soil, the worm castings contain five times more nitrogen, seven times more phosphorus, and 11 times more potassium. They are rich in humic acids and improve the structure of the soil.[2]

To harvest vermi-compost, push the black, decomposed material to one side of the bin, and fill the other side with new, moist garden and kitchen scraps. Then wait several days. The worms will migrate to the freshly filled side of the bin and you can scoop out the finished compost. Make an effort to pick out any remaining worms and return them to the bin.

Photograph 8.4 Worm Box, Peg and Charlie Galbraith

[2] http://lancaster.unl.edu/pest/resources/vermicompost107.shtml

Composting

I have to admit, because of compost's need for water and the scarcity of water in our area, I didn't compost for years and still do so only half-heartedly. Instead, I throw all my kitchen scraps, yard prunings, weeds, and other plant debris into the chicken pen where the hens munch and make manure from it, and till the rest into the soil. I put moldy kitchen scraps into the worm bin. When I need top soil, I simply pull back the mulch layer in the chicken pen and take off the top two inches of soil. This works well for us at Mother Nature Gardens because chickens break down all the waste materials we throw their way into nitrogen-rich manure in a day or two, using only the water they drink. By comparison, compost piles require six to 12 months for the same process, plus regular watering.

Yet, after a couple years, I noticed that the inside of my chicken run looked a lot like a huge, spread-out compost pile. I wanted to gather all those partially broken down materials and I wanted a place to put old, manure-covered straw from the coop. The solution was a simple compost bin created by driving a single pole into the ground 4 feet out from the corner of the coop and placing fencing between the pole and the fencing of the chicken run. This new fenced off area became my compost. Locating the compost immediately next to the chicken run makes it easy for me to compost all the partially decomposed materials from inside the coop (all our kitchen scraps still go to the chickens first for primary decomposition). Because we try to limit our water use to rainwater, the compost bin goes dormant in the hot summer as our precious water is needed elsewhere. During those months, it works more like an organic material holding tank, waiting for the rains to come. Some of these materials get removed in the fall to use on the garden beds for sheet mulching.

However, many people decide to use more full-fledged compost bins, so let's see how they work and what choices you need to make before starting one.

First, to break down effectively, compost needs a roughly half and half mixture of "greens" and "browns," small materials, moisture, air, and time. Green materials are high in nitrogen, break down quickly, and include food scraps, grass clippings, and rotting manure. Brown materials are high in carbon, break down slowly, and include brown leaves, straw, paper, wood chips, and sawdust. If there is too much green material, the compost will get slimy and foul-smelling. If there is too much brown material, the compost will take too long to decompose and require a lot more water to break down. So balance your compost's diet with greens and browns.

Break up woody materials before adding them to your compost pile. Because compost needs to stay consistently moist, not wet, to break down, make sure you can easily reach it with a hose. Compost that stays wet consistently will start to smell bad. Compost, like us, is alive and so it needs air. Turn your pile regularly to get air to the material at the bottom. Then, give it four to 12 months. Because the compost production process takes time, some people have two compost bins: one where they collect materials, and another which is actively breaking materials down into soil.

You can make a compost bin out of anything that will contain materials – posts and fencing or wood slats. Mice will find your compost, mind you. If this bothers you, there are good commercial compost bins that seal very well but have holes for aeration.

 ## Sheet Mulching

The forest builds soil by accumulating years of plant debris, bird poop, decaying insects, and decomposing animals. Sheet mulching works the same way, in an exaggerated and accelerated fashion. It begins with thick layers of organic material that are condensed into a small area, exactly where they will be broken down and used. Think of sheet mulching as a compost pile that is right on top of your garden, saving you from transferring materials from one place to another. Sheet mulch works best if it is implemented in the fall, in alignment with nature's natural decomposition cycle. The organic matter in sheet mulch breaks down from the bottom up, making nutrients available to plants early in the spring.

Photograph 8.5 Sheet Mulching

Steps for Sheet Mulching

1. To begin the sheet mulching process, wet down your designated area.

2. To speed the integration of existing soil with what you are about to add, break up the soil, about 6 inches deep, with a pitchfork, a hoe, a spade, or a tiller. This is the only time we encourage tilling and it's not entirely necessary. We have had sheet mulching success when we skipped this step.

3. Now, spread a layer of manure and then wet it down. Horse owners often have more manure than they know what to do with and are usually glad to let you haul some off. Horse stall waste typically includes manure and nitrogen-rich urine-soaked saw dust or hay. Hay cleaned out from the chicken coop also makes a great manure source for sheet mulching. Avoid cow manure as it tends to contain lots of soil-damaging salts, antibiotics, and growth hormones. Manure adds nitrogen to the soil, the single most important chemical needed for plant growth. If you live in a wet area or wish to plant under pine trees, add wood ash or lime to your sheet mulching layer to neutralize the soil.

4. Then, cover the manure with a layer of cardboard, paperboard, or thick newspaper and dampen this layer. Overlap the edges so that no light penetrates to the layer below. Weed seeds in the manure may germinate with moisture and warmth but the lack of light will quickly kill them. Worms flock to this high carb diet – that's "carb" as in carbon. The layer of paper products attracts, feeds, and produces a thriving worm population.

5. Next, add a 3- to 5-inch layer of leaf material. This layer is your food source for decomposing microorganisms. When sheet mulching in the fall, leaves are easy to find. Often, neighbors will collect them, bag them, and set them on the curb for you. All right, they collect them for the dump, but I have never had anyone bother to stop me when I haul leaves away before the city can get to them. Water this layer.

6. Next, add another multi-inch layer of manure for more nitrogen or an inch layer of compost. Compost breeds within it amazing quantities of microorganisms. More than 5 billion microorganisms for every handful of compost! In our layers of organic materials, compost stimulates decomposition by putting the players onto the field. If you can't afford to buy compost to add to the compost pile don't worry – the decomposing microorganisms will appear just with layers of organic materials. But a little jumpstart never hurts. Dampen this layer.

7. Add another layer of leafy materials if you have them. If you have compost left over, put another layer of that on top. Of course, you know by now to dampen each layer.

8. Top the area off with a layer of mulch and a drink of water. We have successfully used wood mulch and straw in the past. The pile will be tall.

9. Water a few times over the winter and, as spring and summer pass, watch the tall pile start to shrink and integrate into a treasure trove of very rich soil.

In addition to helping grow great vegetables, sheet mulching is wonderful because it costs little or no money. Horse poop, cardboard, green waste, compost, and wood chips are all available for free or at reasonable prices. Gardening is truly an art of making beauty out of waste products.

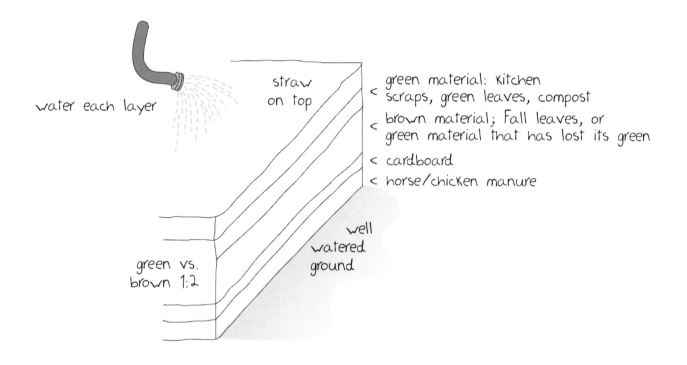

Drawing 8.2 Layers of Sheet Mulch

 Stop Tilling!

Isn't it great when the answer to a problem is "Do less work!" If your soil is particularly hard and suffering, you may decide to work it the very first year you start your garden with a large hoe, pitch fork, or shovel to break it up. If you time things well and prepare for spring planting by sheet mulching in the fall, however, breaking up the soil will not be necessary. Almost all garden annuals grow in the top 6 inches of topsoil. Blame their high maintenance on their shallow root systems. As explained above, sheet mulching breaks down to create nutrient and micororganism-rich topsoil where annuals can flourish.

Many gardeners promote tilling, even double digging, which encourages you to till the soil over 12 inches deep. Breaking up the soil this deep not only requires intense labor, it destroys the natural structure that exists in soil. As mulch and sheet mulching break down, a visible, white web of life called mycelium develops. This fungus structure is necessary because it holds nutrients and water in the soil. Every time you break up the soil, you demolish that structure and it has to recreate itself. Let the life developing in your soil continue to do its work undisturbed. Assist this natural process by adding layers of nutrients on top of the soil with mulch throughout the year, and sheet mulch annually.

Our Home Farms
From Zoe

At MNG, after sheet mulching three seasons in a row and never tilling, we can dig beyond our forearms into the soil before we reach the clay that originally characterized the area. Even with all that nutrient-rich soil available, when we pull up mature tomato plants, some roots spread out as far as 3 feet or more, but go down no deeper than 6 inches. The topsoil holds all the nutrients and moisture under a thick layer of mulch. The plants have no need to grow deep into the subsoil.

We fertilize the plants with a little compost tea or fish emulsion (which can be purchased at most nurseries) to give them a welcome-to-the-neighborhood boost. As the summer passes, the organic matter from mulching and sheet mulching continues to break down from the bottom up, feeding the plants slowly and continually. This replaces the need for fertilizing throughout the summer, as the soil does this for us. Usually, by the end of July, all the fall sheet mulching has broken down completely and we notice plants need a little extra help. Often, nitrogen-rich rains fill this need perfectly.

Exercise 8.1 Building Your Soil

Take a few minutes to consider how you will build soil for your home farm:

1. Will you have a compost bin? Where will it be located? Where will you get leaf waste, green waste, and food waste for your compost? Will all of it come from your own property?

2. Will you have a worm bin? Where will it be located?

3. Will you sheet mulch your garden? What materials will you use and where will you get them? When will you do your sheet mulching?

4. What other steps do you need to consider to build the soil on your property?

Chapter Nine:

Planting the Vegetable Garden and Beyond

Overview

Now that you've prepared fertile growing beds, it's time to plant them! In this chapter, we'll discuss seed sources: heirlooms, hybrids, GMO vegetable varieties, and your own personal seed storage. We'll talk about cool and warm season vegetables to fill your growing space over three seasons. Then, we will address maintenance issues like weeding, fertilizing, and pest control (all watering issues were covered in Chapter Six). We'll learn simple methods to control the temperature in your growing beds at different seasons of the year to maximize and extend your growing season.

While you're reading this information, remember that there are no hard-and-fast rules in growing veggies, only broad tendencies. Each geographic location and piece of land will excel at growing different produce at different times. If you are looking for specific, detailed instructions for all the hundreds of vegetable varieties that exist, we recommend you read the back of your seed packages.

Use this chapter instead as a guide to get you experimenting in your garden, because personal experience with your land is the greatest teacher. You may follow instructions to the letter and still fail to produce a cucumber year after year. Don't take it personally. Instead, understand that your land with its microclimates is simply not ideal for cucumbers. Find what is easy to grow and grow that. Then, take your bumper crop of string beans and make a trade with a friend who grows cucumbers without effort. Again, we are students of the land, continually adapting to what the land teaches us about itself.

Our Home Farms
From Zoe

During our second summer season growing at Mother Nature Gardens, when our soil was still developing, we weren't satisfied with our daily harvest from the garden. Cucumber plants perished and tomato plants, carefully tended, were slow to bear fruit.

Then one day, I went out with my harvest basket hopeful for some produce. I peeked between plants and under leaves until I found a green chile plant with fruit and began to pick. I kept investigating and picking and was amazed at the amount of produce hidden in that one plant. I then visited other chile plants with the same results – they were all bursting with peppers. That day I harvested bushels of green chiles from plants I had almost forgotten in a garden we were starting to lose hope in.

It dawned on me that, of course, green chiles would grow effortlessly in my garden. New Mexico is renowned for its red and green chile cuisine. Long ago, farmers discovered New Mexico as the perfect climate and soil for this spicy vegetable. So chile dishes have been an important part of the local culture that developed directly from a connection with the earth.

Photograph 9.1 Chile Harvest

Selecting and Saving Seed

 ## Heirloom Seeds

Heirloom plants have pure genetics, which produces fertile seed. Heirloom varieties were developed by farmers who carefully selected their seed for desired outcomes, such as sweeter fruit and drought- or pest-resistant plants. The farmers then saved their seeds generation after generation. Thousands of varieties of tomatoes, for example, grow well under a diversity of conditions and produce different colors, flavors, and shapes of fruit. Diversity supports food security and connects people to history and tradition through their food, so we encourage efforts to use and preserve heirloom vegetable varieties.

 ## Hybrid Seeds

Agriculturists hybridize vegetables by cross-pollinating two varieties, producing a third variety that contains desired characteristics of both parents. Hybrid vegetables typically produce seeds that are not fertile. If the seed is fertile, it may not produce plants true to the hybrid characteristics, or the plants produced may not bear the characteristics of the parent plants. Each generation lowers fertility rates. If your intent is to save vegetable seeds from year to year, don't buy hybrid varieties. Both heirloom and hybrid seeds can be certified organic and packages are usually marked to identify whether the seeds are heirloom or hybrid, and whether they are organic. The only types of seed that are not marked in this way are Genetically Modified Organism (GMO) seeds, which, as we will explain below, are not organic, and do not produce offspring that you can plant.

 ## Genetically Modified Organisms

GMO (genetically modified organism) varieties of vegetables have been genetically altered in a laboratory at the DNA level of the plant cell to include genes from other types of organisms, including animals. The goal is to produce a plant with specific characteristics, such as pest resistance. GMO plants do not produce fertile seeds, so farmers who use GMO seeds must buy seeds year after year. These seeds can cross-pollinate with heirloom seeds and contaminate them, such that the offspring plants from the heirloom seeds no longer produce fertile seeds. Not only does this wipe out the genetic history and future continuation of an heirloom crop with a gust of cross-pollinating wind, but GMO seeds are patented. So currently, until laws shift toward more justice and security for all, the company that owns the rights to the GMO-patented seed can sue an heirloom farmer for having the company's GMO genes in the heirloom farmer's crop without having paid for them. In this way, these companies are attempting to establish an agricultural monopoly.

Studies indicate the consumption of GMO produce may be linked to cancer and other diseases. The sale of GMO seeds and produce is illegal in many developed countries, like all of Europe and Japan, because of the associated health concerns and the threat of eliminating a diverse, self-sustaining seed stock that keeps power in the hands of the farmer. The United States has yet to require full disclosure of genetic tampering with food or seeds, so when you go to the grocery store you may not know whether you are buying GMO or non-GMO produce. However, all produce that is certified organic is non-GMO. So, if you buy organic produce you can be sure you are not buying the fruits of GMO seeds.

Efforts by very powerful seed companies to own patents for heirloom seed varieties and make available only a handful of hybrid or GMO veggie varieties should alarm us into action, from the seed choices we make in the spring, the food we pick off the shelf in the grocery store, to the choices we make in the voting booth. A few companies now own 80% of the world's vegetable seed varieties. That puts an enormous amount of power for control of our food security and safety into the hands of a very few. As home farmers, we must choose to take back our power and grow healthy, fertile strains of food. We believe in the importance of buying seeds from conscious businesses that want to help people cultivate healthy food, not control our food supply as well as the agricultural economy by using an imbalance of power.

> ## Helpful Notes: Seed Sources
>
> As mentioned earlier, sources for hierloom seeds include: rareseeds. com and landrethseeds.com. Seedsavers.com is a non-profit dedicated to saving and sharing heirloom seeds. Cooksgarden.com, parkseed.com, organicseedpeople.com, and naturalgardening.com are sources for organic seeds. Nativeseeds.org is another non-profit dedicated to saving and sharing native seeds in the southwest and northwest Mexico.

 ## Saving Your Own Seed

We would not exist if our ancestors had not saved seed from one year to plant again the next year. Saving your own seed stock is rewarding and vital for a future of affordable, diverse food, but you must know the limitations involved.

Hybrid plants, as mentioned before, produce infertile seed, which should not be collected. Also some popular garden veggies, including squash, cucumbers, melon, parsley, cabbage, chard, broccoli, mustard greens, celery, spinach, cauliflower, kale, radish, beets, onion, and basil are open pollinators that can cross with other species within their family. You need an isolated gene pool to cultivate pure seed, and you need a large gene pool (like a half an acre of cauliflower) to keep genetics strong year after year. This would be impossible for most of our readers and not in alignment with all the growing techniques for small pieces of land that we have described so far. You can try to save and use seeds from organic veggies you buy at the grocery store, but you often can't tell whether these vegetables were hybrids and you definitely can't determine their genetic purity.

The good candidates for seed saving include heirloom garlic, beans, tomatoes, lettuce, peppers, and marigolds. When choosing your mother plant, choose a disease-free plant with qualities you desire, like the most flavorful or largest fruit or the pepper plant that survived when you went out of town and forgot to turn on the watering system. Always harvest mature seed. For example, a tomato ready to eat contains seeds that aren't yet ripe. You must allow the fruit and seed to fully mature.

For beans, lettuce, peppers, and flowers, allow the seed to ripen and begin to dry on the plant. Don't wait too long or you will lose seed to birds and wind. Shake the pods out in a paper bag to collect the seeds. Allow them to complete the drying process on a paper towel in a dry, well-ventilated area. Store in labeled, dated glass jars or envelopes.

Tomatoes require a wet method of collection. Scoop the seed mass out and place it in a small amount of water in a glass jar. Allow this mixture to sit for two to four days. Stir daily. In a couple of days, the fertile seed will sink to the bottom while the undesirable seeds will float to the top. Screen off the top pulp and then the water from the good seeds. Allow them to complete the drying process on a paper towel in a well-ventilated area. Store seeds in a labeled, dated glass jar or envelope.[3]

Cool and Warm Season Vegetables

You can divide garden vegetable into two categories, those that grow best when the weather is cool, like leafy greens, and warm season vegetables that thrive in the long days of summer, like tomatoes. How long each of these seasons last, and when they start and stop, will depend on your geographic location and, as weather patterns change, year-to-year temperature differences.

In areas that have four distinct seasons, grow your first batch of cool season veggies in late winter and early spring. Later in the chapter we will discuss cold frames and row covers to help protect veggies through these chillier times. Another round of cool season seeds can go in the ground in most places when temperatures turn cooler after the summer growing season, in late August through September. You'll harvest these in the late fall and beginning of winter.

Warm season veggies go in the ground in April and May, just as you pull out your onions. They are ready to harvest in the late summer and fall. This year, we experimented with waiting until June to plant our warm season crops. We had noticed during previous summers that our veggies required lots of watering

---

[3] http://urbanext.Illinois.edu/horthints

during the blazing hot months of July and August but seemed stunted in their growth. We thought we could save a month of water if we waited. It worked well, although our tomatoes were late to fruit and slow to redden.

If you plant in late winter, late spring, and late summer or early fall, you can enjoy fresh garden vegetables three out of the four seasons of the year. Even with three-season gardening, however, you will notice waves of vegetable harvests. Spring offers a large quantity of leafy and flower veggies like broccoli and cauliflower. Plant smaller batches of seeds monthly to spread out your harvest. I notice a lull of fresh vegetables in the first half of summer after cool season crops have bolted and warm season vegetables are still developing. Fortunately, many fruiting trees, like apricot and peach, as well as strawberries and wild berries, ripen during this time to fill in the gap. From late summer into fall, we tend to eat the "fruits" of our vegetable plants, like tomatoes, zucchini, eggplants, and peppers. In the fall, we harvest winter squash and potatoes and are nursing our next batch of leafy greens.

Our Home Farms
From Zoe

In central New Mexico, we have mild winters and intensely hot summers. At Mother Nature Gardens, we can grow almost all winter long with row covers. In fact, the more we garden in the arid Southwest, the more we focus on extending our cool season growth. Last year, we seeded in early February and were eating fresh salads daily by the end of that month. Cool weather means less evaporation, thus less watering, and very little challenge with insects. Conversely, in the warm season, we need to monitor vegetables much more closely for dehydration and pest patrol.

Photograph 9.2 Lettuce Growing at Mother Nature Gardens

Helpful Notes:

Examples of Cold Season Vegetables

- Lettuces
- Spinach
- Chard
- Cauliflower
- Broccoli
- Chives
- Cilantro
- Carrots
- Beets
- Spring onions
- Radishes

- Brussels sprouts
- Peas

Examples of Warm Season Vegetables

- Tomatoes/tomatillos
- Peppers and chilies
- Eggplants
- Summer and winter squashes
- Sunflowers
- Cucumbers
- Watermelons and cantaloupes
- Green beans
- Beans
- Corn

Helpful Notes:

A Word about Garlic

Garlic tastes delicious, fortifies the immune system for all-around better health, and is easy to grow. Buy *organic* garlic bulbs from a garlic grower, your local plant store, or a grocery store. You must choose organic garlic from a grocery store because, aside from the dangers of GMO varieties, non-organic growers spray bulbs so they won't sprout. This makes their shelf life longer and it makes them useless as seed stock.

Split the bulbs into cloves. Plant the cloves 6 inches deep around Halloween. Water and cover the bulbs with soil. Harvest them when the green tops die back in early summer.

Photograph 9.3 Garlic Grown at MNG

Helpful Notes:

Sources for Planning Your Garden, and Buying Plants and Grow Lights

Gardeners.com has a full drag-and-drop resource for planning a kitchen garden online. Naturalgardening.com is the oldest certified organic nursery in the U.S. Led-Grow-Master.com is a great source for grow lights of all kinds.

Methods to Extend Your Growing Season

 **Row Covers**

At Mother Nature Gardens our ability to plant seeds directly in the ground the 1st of February and eat homegrown greens late the next month is thanks to the use of a very simple row cover. Row covering is a breathable, white, synthetic cloth used for covering crops. You can buy it over the Internet in bulk or at a nursery by the yard. Remay, a brand name row cover, makes two thicknesses: a single ply for shading in the summer and a double ply for winter protection. Double ply raises internal temperatures six degrees above outdoor temperatures, and it shelters leaves from descending frost. Row cover fabric can be purchased at gardeners.com and many other suppliers.

To cover your rows properly, you will need structural arches that span across your garden beds like ribs. Many rib options exist. At Mother Nature Gardens, one year we harvested willow branches that we stuck in one side of the row and bent over the top and into the other side. They worked well, you can't beat the price, and ours even sprouted willow leaves! The rough surface, however, punctured and damaged our row cover.

We used and promoted the use of PVC piping until we learned about the extreme toxicity of vinyl at every stage of its production. Not wanting to support more pollution, we currently use U-shaped pieces of rebar.

Starting Seeds Indoors

Some plants are happiest when they begin their life in a garden bed as a seedling, instead of a seed. Rather than buying plant starts from a nursery, you can start the plants yourself We do this typically with summer crops like tomatoes, eggplant, and peppers. Start your seeds indoors six weeks before you plan to plant them outdoors. Nurseries have lots of options for seed-starting kits but plastic starter pots saved from last year or egg cartons work well. The trick with starting seeds indoors is keeping them constantly moist. We like the start-up kits with covers that help retain moisture. We avoid kits with peat moss since peat moss is not a sustainably-harvested resource. Led-grow-master.com is a great source for any type of grow light.

Photograph 9.4 Row Cover Ribs Pulled Aside with Row Cover

Summer Shade for Veggies

Plants that enjoy full sun in most climates still appreciate a reprieve from the intense Southwestern sun in the heat of the summer. Even with its roots in wet ground, a vegetable can look wilted in the middle of the day because it cannot pull in enough water from the ground to make up for the amount of water transpiring through its leaves. Shading the west side of your veggie bed from afternoon sun will lessen plant stress and the need for water.

A simple way to shade your garden, especially as it is getting established, is to replace your double-ply row cover for cool season warmth with single-ply row cover, made for summer shading. Alternatively, try moving your double-ply just to the west side of the row-cover ribs. This works until the plants grow above the height of your ribs. Prepare for this transition by planting sunflowers on the west edge of your beds for beautiful and effortless afternoon shade.

We have also tried, with reasonable success, strips of sheets (2-to 3-feet tall and as long or as short as the area you are shading) stapled to stakes with a staple gun or attached with plastic cinch-ties on the west side and above planted areas. Whatever material you use as shade cloth, it helps if it is semi-permeable so it won't catch the wind. So poke some holes in your sheets. Creating shade for your garden shouldn't require more than a few dollars and some creativity.

 ## Exercise 9.1 Planning Your Crops

What crops will you grow when in your garden?

a. Will you plant **cold season** crops in the late winter and early spring? Which ones and when? Will they be from seed or from starter plants? And if they are from starter plants, will you grow these yourself indoors, or buy them?

1A Planning Cold Season Crops

Crop	Date to Plant Outside	From Seed or Starter Plant?	If from starter plant, buy or raise it?	If raising starter plants, when to start indoors?

How will you protect your cold season crops from getting too cold? Will you use row covers or some other type of protection?

b. Will you plant **warm season** crops in the summer? Which ones and when? Will they be from seed or from starter plants? And if they are from starter plants, will you grow these yourself indoors, or buy them?

B Planning Warm Season Crops

Crop	Date to Plant Outside	From Seed or Starter Plant?	If from starter plant, buy or raise it?	If raising starter plants, when to start indoors?

How will you protect your warm season crops from getting too much sun? Will you use row covers or some other type of shade devices?

c. Will you plant a **second season** of cold season crops in the fall? Which ones and when? Will they be from seed or from starter plants? And if they are from starter plants, will you grow these yourself indoors, or buy them?

C Planning a Second Season of Cold Crops

Crop	Date to Plant Outside	From Seed or Starter Plant?	If from starter plant, buy or raise it?	If raising starter plants, when to start indoors?

How will you protect your cold season crops from getting too cold? Will you use row covers or some other type of protection?

Maintaining Your Garden

 ## Overview

In addition to sheltering it from intense, full sun during the day, a summer garden also needs weeding, fertilizing, and insect and disease control. The need for these maintenance tasks will be less prevalent as your soil develops year after year and beds become more full and diverse. However, in the first few years especially, monitor your garden throughout the summer months with these continued care guidelines.

 ## Weeding

To control weeds, start with an environment that does not encourage them. Interplant your garden in layers of growth, as described in Chapter Eight. Competition with lots of desired veggies will minimize available space for weeds to sprout. Then, mulch heavily around your desired plants (making sure not to let the mulch touch the base of young plants). Remember, pioneering weed species thrive in bare soil.

A plant becomes a weed when its presence outweighs its value. To lessen the work required for weeding, try to learn the name and value of any plant that comes up in your garden. Just because you didn't plant it does not mean it's not useful. The resourceful as well as the lazy gardener should spend time learning which weeds are edible.

Helpful Notes: Edible Weeds

- Dandelions – Young leaves eaten fresh
- Lamb's quarters – Leaves eaten fresh or cooked
- Plaintain – Young leaves eaten fresh, mature leaves cooked like spinach
- Purslane – leaves, stems, and flowers fresh or cooked like spinach
- Chicory – Young leaves eaten fresh
- Nettles – Leaves cooked like spinach
- Amaranth also known as pigweed – Leaves cooked like spinach
- Burdock – Young stalks used in place of artichoke hearts. Roots used in soups and casseroles

When you do identify an undesirable weed, pull it when the plant is young, before it develops deep roots. Don't let weeds stay in your garden until it's a serious chore to take them out. Instead, pull weeds here and there while you check on your plants, on your evening constitutional trip around the garden, or as you water. If you let weeds go until they are too well-rooted to pull, use a tool to pry them up or cut the plant at its base if pulling it out doesn't work. What is important is that you do not let a weed start to flower and seed. A single weed that goes to seed can cause an out-of-control rash of that weed the next year. If you find weeds taking over your growing space, make your growing space smaller next year and include more perennials in your bed. Keep the rest of your land under 4 inches of mulch until you are ready to expand. Four inches of mulch will prevent most weeds from popping up. If some still manage to work their way through, they are easier to pull out of mulch than from bare ground.

On our home farms, the weeds we pull serve as fodder for chickens. Fodder is green material collected from surrounding environments for animals on the farm. Knowing this motivates me further to weed, because I am serving two functions at once: weeding and feeding. We send any goatheads or Russian thistle to the green recycling center because eating the pokey seed may injure our chickens.

Fertilizing with Compost Tea

Soil that was sheet mulched in the fall should not require much additional fertilizing throughout the growing season. If you didn't get around to sheet mulching last year or you feel your plants need an extra boost, there are healthy and inexpensive methods for augmenting your soil during the growing season. You can buy fish emulsion from your local nursery, or try making a batch of compost tea.

To make compost tea, fill a 5-gallon bucket with water. Then, add a permeable sack filled with compost, vermi-compost from your worm bin, or chicken manure. If you can't find a sack, just add the nutrients directly into the water. The helpful microorganisms in the compost and vermi-compost will multiple quickly. Chicken manure contains concentrated amounts of nitrogen that will burn a plant if it is applied directly. Processing chicken manure into "manure tea," however, makes the nitrogen safe and available.

Keep the bucket covered and stir it vigorously twice a day. The process of creating compost tea depends on stirring, which aerates the water and activates interaction among micro-organisms. You also can use an aquarium aerator to continually aerate the tea. After a week or two of processing, mix the tea with water, one-part tea to three-parts water. Apply compost tea around the roots of tired-looking plants and watch their appreciation in the following days. You can also put compost tea into a spray bottle and spray directly on leaves to form a micro-organism shield that helps with leaf-borne diseases like blight.

Drawing 9.1 Making Compost Tea

 Disease and Pest Control

We have already gone to great lengths to control disease and pests by creating a good environment for strong plants. The healthy soil we have built helps maintain each plant's vibrant health so it can fight off diseases and pests. Mulched beds and shade structures reduce plant stress. A high diversity of plants reduces the risk of pest infestation and welcomes beneficial insects that keep the pest-insect population in balance. A daily constitutional trip around the garden to observe what is happening will keep you abreast of any unwanted pest presence. Pests still appear, however, and sometimes their damage seems to occur very quickly.

When a plant is unhealthy, look at the environment first. In medicine, this is called terrain theory versus germ theory. Is the plant adequately covered with soil? Is it stressed by sun or another nearby plant? Is it stressed because it is isolated and overexposed? Is the plant's soil healthy? Is it getting efficient water?

Our Home Farms
From Zoe

Adding more life to out-compete unwanted life is always preferable to focusing on the problem. We have a peach tree in our back yard that suffered from an attack of aphids. Instead of spraying the bugs and focusing on the problem, we sent the neighbor kids on a hunt for ladybugs to transfer to the tree. They found over a dozen, learned that ladybugs eat aphids, and had a great time. When I noticed songbirds feeding on the aphids, I sprinkled the ground below the tree with chicken feed to attract more birds to its branches. We sprayed the leaves with compost tea. The micro-organisms in the tea form a living shield, making it more difficult for the aphids to penetrate the leaf surface. As a longer-term solution, we increased diversity by planting the base of the tree with strong-scented herbs like rue, yarrow, tansy, and garlic chives. The tree lived through the aphid attack fine.

Common plant diseases include blight, curly top, and blossom end rot.

- Blight is airborne, affects tomatoes in particular, and causes white powdery buildup on leaves. Apply compost tea to the leaves in the early summer at the first sign of blight.

- Curly top is a fungus that can turn a beautiful tomato plant into a sick, curly-leafed mess in a day or two. Once you see a victim of curly top, you will know what it is. The leaves simply curl up all over the plant. If curly top has taken over a tomato plant, remove the plant and spray neighboring plants with compost tea. Look for rocket ship mustards growing on your land in winter. This plant, although edible when it is young, harbors the curly top virus.

- Blossom end rot shows up as browned fruit at the bottom of a tomato or a pepper. This indicates calcium deficiency in the soil and can be cured with an application of lime or bone meal, and by watering with rainwater.

Common pests include aphids, squash bugs, cutworms, flea beetles, and pill bugs.

- Aphids are tiny bugs that collect in masses and particularly enjoy the brassica family (cauliflower, Brussels sprouts, and broccoli). Companion plant brassica varieties with aphid deterrents like basil, garlic, and peppers. Ladybugs eat aphids, so focus on attracting ladybugs. The umbilifera family, including yarrow, Queen Ann's lace, and carrots, attracts ladybugs. You can also spray a plant that is infected with aphids with a mild soap and water solution.

- The law with squash bugs is to plant squash plants after the typical reproduction cycle for squash bugs ends in late June. Plant your squash plants after the Fourth of July.

- Pill bugs devour young plants at their base. To deter them, we keep organic matter away from the base of the plant. Put a large aluminum can, cut out at both ends, around the base of each young plant. However, sometimes it's hard to control pill bugs, and you may lose some plants to them.

> ### Helpful Notes: Natural Pest Control Products
>
> If you feel you must use pest control products, please make sure they won't create toxicity in your garden for bees, humans, pets, and the environment. Sources for natural pest control supplies include plantnatural.com, saferbrand.com, arbico-organics.com, and gardensalive.com.

Introduction to Lunar Planting

People have been planting according to the cycles of the moon since there was agriculture. Farmers close to the earth and without electricity noticed how plant growth fluctuated predictably with the moon phases. They also noticed that crop success varied according to what phase the moon was in when the crops were planted. Thousands of years of research can't be included here, of course.

However, an overview is still interesting and helpful. I use *The Farmer's Almanac* and a lunar calendar to keep my garden activities aligned with the expanding and contracting energy of the moon. The moon completes one waxing and waning cycle in about 28 days and four phases. Half of that time, the first and second phase, the moon waxes to full. During the second half of the moon cycle, phases two and three, it wanes to a dark moon.

The water, nutrients, and growth in a plant follow the waxing moon by moving from the roots up to the top of the plant. Because of this, fruits weigh more, have higher nutritional value, and seem tastier when harvested during the phase of the full moon. Herbalists choose to gather leaves and flowers when the moon is full because their medicine is most potent at this time.

As the moon wanes, water and nutrients in the plant get pulled from the leaves, flowers, and fruit into the roots. Predictably, this is when root growth occurs.

Each phase of the moon is associated with a different aspect of the plant's growth and structure: first phase, leaf; second phase, fruit; third phase, root; and fourth phase, rest. If your final harvest is the leaf of the plant, like spinach and kale, plant in the first moon phase. If you want an abundance of fruit, like eggplants and tomatoes, plant in the second phase of the moon. In the third phase of the moon, plant root crops like turnips and onions when root growth is most encouraged. Let the soil rest during phase four as you focus on tool repair, building projects, and your own rest.

 Exercise 9.2 Your Lunar Gardening

Are there a couple of simple changes you could make to when and how you farm that would bring your activities more in sync with the phases of the moon? What would those be?

Your Notes

Birds & Bees

Once your property is supporting plant life to help feed and heal you, the next step is for it to support beneficial creatures that can do the same. On the home farm, chickens and honeybees provide tremendous food, medicinal, and symbiotic benefits while taking up very little space.

Chapter Ten:

Keeping Chickens

Overview

This chapter will help you get started keeping chickens, even if you are a total beginner. You will learn the ins and outs of a chicken's life, and some of the different varieties of chickens you can raise. You'll also gain insight into your biggest investment as a chicken owner: your coop. Finally, we'll talk about buying chickens and how you can care for them at any age.

Why Keep Chickens?

The first step in planning for chickens is to make sure you want them. Why does anyone want to keep chickens? First, they play a very important role in the farm system. Chickens eat and break down a wider range of nutrients than we can and turn them into food we can eat (eggs and meat). They go crazy for bugs! They'll fight over a cockroach. This makes them chemical- free pest controllers. In the fall, your chickens can clean your spent beds of pest infestations.

Chickens create a closed production/waste/production loop because they are natural recyclers. They eat carrot peels and weeds, plants infested with insects, and stale bread. They are on-site green-waste decomposers. They take those human-inedible things and use them to produce human-edible (and delicious) proteins, like eggs and chicken meat. They provide a clean, local source of protein, moving our individual plots of land closer towards sustainability. Raising chickens at home provides higher quality, fresher eggs and meat (if you choose to harvest the hens eventually) than you can find in any grocery store because of the quality of the food you feed them, and the home you provide for them. At Mother Nature Gardens, some mornings, we crack eggs in the frying pan that are still warm from the chicken, and their vibrant orange yolks taste like cheese.

Chickens constantly produce another farm-valuable by-product: manure. Chicken manure is a nitrogen-potent, abundant fertilizer that comes free with every chicken you purchase. It's so powerful, in fact, that in order to avoid burning your plants, you must process the chicken manure as part of sheet mulching, composting (for three to six months), or in manure tea (the brother of compost tea- see Chapter Eight).

As they hunt, scratch, dive for bugs, and cackle to each other and to you, chickens entertain even the coldest heart. In our Peace Corps village in Zambia, where we had no electricity or phones or even movement to look at besides tree branches swaying in the wind, chickens were like television. For children they are a special pleasure.

Of course, chickens require regular care and become another living part of your immediate surroundings. At Mother Nature Gardens, we buy feed once a month and use it to supplement the kitchen scraps and fodder we collect for our chickens. We clean out the coop and chicken pen and care for the birds and the flock. Yet they pay for themselves in spades for all the life they contribute to our home farm.

A Chicken's Lifecycle

I like to begin talking about raising chickens by a discussion of the chicken herself. Once mature, a hen will lay an egg a day almost daily for the first two years.

When she is ready to raise chicks, she'll go broody, which means she will sit on her eggs until they hatch. Of course, in order for the eggs to hatch, they need to be fertilized, which means that you need a rooster. However, the hen will not realize this distinction: she will go broody whether or not her eggs are fertilized. Note that this happens at different ages for different types of hens, and varies with each individual hen as well.

While broody, she won't come out of the coop except to eat a little bit and will become quite cranky about letting you harvest her eggs (if she were a human, we'd call it "broody syndrome" and might have a pill to clear the symptoms). She will incubate her eggs for three weeks, and, if the eggs are fertilized, a chick will hatch from approximately 75% of her eggs. You will not know the sex of the chicks until later – male chickens will begin to grow a cock's comb at the age of about 3 to 6 months, and female chickens will not. When buying chicks, you can buy them sexed, that is, identified as male or female.

As a teen, the cock's comb identifies the bird as a cockerel. Young hens are known as pullets through their first year, even though they begin to lay after around 6 months, depending on the variety. Although a hen will lay eggs most consistently during her first two years, she will keep laying throughout her life (the average chicken's lifespan is 5 to 7 years), but quantity will go down each year. Chickens can live up to 20 years.

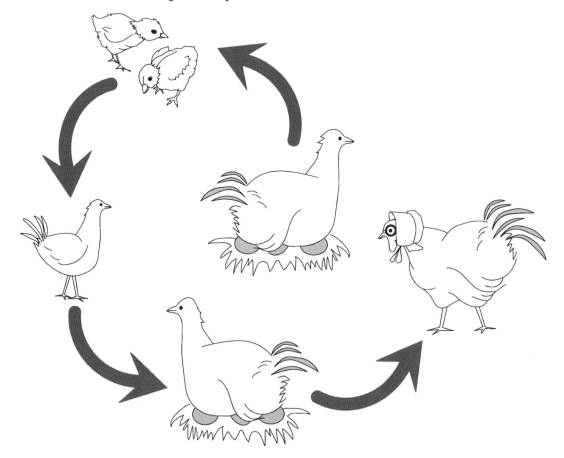

Drawing 10.1 Lifecycle of a Chicken

Photograph 10.1 A Hen on Her Nest- Courtesy of Sharon Austin

What Do Chickens Need to be Healthy and Happy?

To best care for your chickens, assess and plan for their needs before you buy them. Chickens need a run in which to scratch, dust themselves, feed, and enjoy the outdoors. They need a coop to get out of the weather, lay their eggs, and roost for the evenings. They need shade from the sun in the hot months, shelter from the rain, and protection from winds and cold during the winter. If they don't have natural shelter from afternoon sun in the summer, create it with fencing or place your coop along the west side of their pen so the coop itself will block the afternoon sun. In Chapter Three, we discussed success by proximity. Since chickens create much traffic from the kitchen to the pen (scraps out and eggs in), I like to place chicken pens as close as reasonably possible to the kitchen.

Food and Water

Chickens are omnivores, so they will eat just about anything. Like us, they need variety in their diet that provides them with protein, fats, carbohydrates, vitamins, and minerals. The amount of food chickens need depends on the breed, their stage of development, and the season. A full-sized hen requires about 4 ounces of food a day, half of which should be grain (that's a large handful), and the rest should be kitchen scraps. For the four chickens we currently have at MNG, we buy a 50-pound bag of scratch food for $18 every six weeks. We get at least eight dozen eggs in that same period of time. Eight dozen good quality eggs at the grocery store, at $3.50 a carton, would cost $28. So raising chickens is cost-effective.

In addition, I feed them all my yard waste as well as fodder (like elm leaves, buds, or seeds) from the gardens. They love spring greens as much as we do. You can also use a feeder and allow the birds to eat as much as they want.

Just like for every other living thing, daily access to clean water is important for hens to stay healthy. Check water supply daily. At Mother Nature Gardens, we invested in a 5-gallon watering device. It was a little pricey but worth it for the freedom it gives us from refilling their water every day. Once we raised the watering unit on blocks so it was at the chicken's head level and away from their scratching feet, the water stayed clean and lasted all week before we needed to refill it. Even if you have a watering unit, it's important to check the water every day in case it gets tipped over, emptied faster than you thought it would, or clogged. When we go out of town for more than a single night, we always have someone who can check in on our chickens. Sometimes they are happy to take pay in eggs!

Photograph 10.2 A Chicken Feeder

Photograph 10.3 Chicken Watering Unit

Helpful Notes: What Chickens Should Not Eat:

- Apple seeds, because they contain traces of cyanide

- Raw meat

- Rotten or moldy food

- Sugared cereals or salty chips

 ## A Clean Shelter and Run

Chickens are a good choice for many mini-farms because they do not need a great amount of space. (Rabbits and ducks also make good mini-farm animals if you wish to research other protein options). Each bird in your flock needs a minimum of 4 square feet in the coop and at least 6 square feet in the run. (We will discuss coops in detail later on in this chapter.) Because hens usually prefer to be outside, having a large enough run is more important than having a large coop. If you have a very small space for your chickens, try raising bantam chickens. In relation to their small size, a bantam needs only 2 square feet for the coop, and 4 square feet for the run. As you experiment with raising different numbers of chickens, watch for signs of overcrowding, such as pecking and fighting. We have had flocks that were too small and flocks that got overcrowded. Through trial and error, Mother Nature Gardens keeps six healthy chickens in a 300 square foot run. This is much more space than the minimum recommended, but we like having low-maintenance, happy hens.

Healthy birds require a clean environment. Rake out coop straw at least once a week. Clean out the laying boxes twice a month. Clean out all organic material once a year. Store the removed material in your compost pile or put it directly on your garden beds in the winter, or on fallow beds during the growing season. Have straw bales on hand to replace old straw when you clean out your run and coop. A layer of straw in the chickens run is also very important. It gives the chickens something to scratch, which makes them endlessly happy. Feed stores usually sell straw bales, and prices vary ($5 to $10 a bale) depending on your area and the season. Lay clean straw, shredded paper, or clothes in the coop after cleaning. These habits will protect against odor and disease.

Companionship

Chickens are social animals and thrive in flocks of three or more for healthy chickens. To determine how many chickens to keep, look at space available, food availability (how much chicken feed you can afford), and how many eggs you want a day. In general, all kinds of chicken varieties will get along living together as long as their needs are well met.

 # Special Care for Sick Chickens

Prevention of disease with good animal husbandry is the lion's share of caring for your hens: clean food and water; clean coop and the correct number of chickens. If a bird does become injured or sick, isolate that hen from the rest of the flock until she returns to good health. If the hen has a disease or pest, she may spread it to other birds if she is not separated, and if she has an injury, other chickens will peck at her open sore so that it doesn't get a chance to heal. If illness does occur, contact your agricultural extension office for help. You can also use many of the same herbal remedies that work for humans – like sage tea if a hen is showing cold symptoms (like coughing and gurgling phlegm).

 # Special Care for Chicks

During the first two to three months of their lives, chicks need special care if they are not with their mama. Because they cannot regulate their own body heat, they require a heat lamp to stay warm. A 25- to 40-watt bulb works well for this. You will know the chicks' environment is too cold if they are huddled beneath the bulb and it is too hot if they are backed against a wall away from it. They also require special chick 'Start and Grow' food (which you should be able to purchase at a local feed store), and this needs to be available to them at all times, along with their water. A brooder is a large boxed area with a light for keeping chicks isolated and safe. Remember, a good mama minds her chicks because baby chicks can be tasty prey for hawks, cats, raccoons, and even other full-grown hens.

Since chicks do require special care, raising chicks may be a challenging place to start if you have never kept chickens before. We recommend you start with pullets or hens the first year and try raising chicks down the line when you have become accustomed to being a chicken owner. If you want more information about chick incubation and hatching, mypetchicken.com has a free eBook on their website.

 ## The Rap on Roosters

A rooster has a few characteristic behaviors that include crowing, breeding, and protecting the flock. The crowing habit makes them illegal in most neighborhoods, even where hens are welcome. Fortunately, chickens do not require a rooster to lay delicious eggs that are ready for you to eat. But having a rooster around is necessary for chickens to produce fertile eggs that will hatch chicks.

Photograph 10.4 A Rooster

A rooster's ability to guard the flock is his most endearing quality, second to his good looks. If you have problems with neighborhood cats or raccoons, a rooster is great to have around. Overly aggressive roosters, however, can attack humans entering the pen to provide food and water. One rooster on our farm grew up to become so mean, we went out to water our hens every day carrying a four-foot steel rod to keep the rooster's clawed side-kicks far from our flesh. He soon ended up on our dinner plates.

Choosing Your Chickens

Chickens come in all kinds of colors, sizes, heights, habits, and hairdos. Just as they have with dogs, humans have bred chickens for particular climates, diets, and situations. And just like dog breeds, some chicken species have strange genetic adaptations, like feathered feet, midget legs, bald heads, or an Elvis-like bouffant of head feathers.

With so many choices, you must know what you want from a bird before you select your breeds – high egg production and/or meat, resilience to heat and/ or cold, tendency to become or not to become broody, ability to get along with many other varieties, docility or friendliness, a bold breed that can fight off your six neighborhood cats, or a fancy variety that can entertain at parties. Shop the local agriculture co-ops and feed stores to see what breeds are available to you. At our local feed stores the following five breeds were most commonly available for purchase.

A Few Common Household Breeds of Chicken

Araucana

- Egg color and frequency: blue/green, medium frequency
- Characteristics: friendly, regularly goes broody

Buff Orpington

- Egg color and frequency: light brown, medium frequency
- Characteristics: friendly and docile, regularly goes broody

Australorps

- Egg color and frequency: brown, high frequency
- Characteristics: friendly and docile, average brooder

Rhode Island Red

- Egg color and frequency: brown, high frequency
- Characteristics: can be aggressive, seldom goes broody, can handle cold temperatures.

Barred/Plymouth Rock

- Egg color and frequency: brown, high frequency
- Characteristics: Friendly, easy to handle, seldom goes broody.

There are endless resources about chicken breeds on the Internet, although we like backyardchickens.com best. They have a resource that allows you to search for breeds with selected characteristics.

Photograph 10.5 Araucana-Courtesy of Daniel Jaecks

Photograph 10.6 Buff Orpington

Photograph 10.7 Black Astrolorph

Photograph 10.8 Road Island Red

Photograph 10.9 Barred Rock

When to Purchase and Where

Many people prefer to buy hens as pullets (chickens are less than a year old), rather than buying chicks. Pullets are sold when they are 3 months or so old, and typically begin laying at around 6 months. They are more immune to predators than chicks, and sex can be more guaranteed so you know you are buying hens and not roosters. Older hens will attack and kill chicks that aren't their own, so chicks must be raised separately from the mature flock. Often local feed stores sell chicks, or you can purchase them at a nearby hatchery. You can also purchase chicks online and have them shipped to you.

Chicken Shelters

 # Portable vs. Stationary Coops vs. Free Roaming

There are three different ways to contain, or not to contain, your chickens: in a stationary coop; in a portable coop (called a "chicken tractor"); or free roaming in your yard with a safe, weather-protected place for them to roost at night.

Photograph 10.10 Example of a Chicken Tractor- Courtesy of Frances Deters, thechickwagon.com

Helpful Notes: Pros and Cons of Different Types of Chicken Shelters

Portable

Pros:

- Moves chickens to living feed
- Distributes fertilizer around your property
- Helps to create new garden beds
- Can be moved or stay in the same spot

Cons:

- Not easy to use with non-standard-shaped growing beds
- Difficult to move onto established beds
- Can't move them on top of any plants you don't want eaten

Stationary

Pros:

- Predictability
- Can be larger than a chicken tractor
- Soil becomes compost source

Cons:

- Almost all food needs to be brought into the pen

Free Roaming

Pros:

- Happy chickens
- Maximizes chickens' access to bugs and weeds

Cons:

- Wreaks havoc on gardens
- Chickens may get out over your walls
- Your chickens may end up roosting anywhere
- Not as easy to protect your chickens from dogs, raccoons, and other predators

Alternative: Try evening outings as an alternative to chicken tractors or free roaming. At dusk, the chickens will effortlessly return to the coop to roost.

 ## The Coop

Chicken shelters basically need four walls and a ceiling with, as we have discussed earlier, a minimum of 4 square feet in the coop per bird. For example, a 5- by 7-foot coop will hold eight birds comfortably.

When you start raising hens, a coop will be your most costly investment, so use materials you already have and/or recycled materials when possible. Chicken coops are great for experimenting with alternative building methods like cob and cob slip, even strawbale. The smartest coop I've seen was a recovered Tuff Shed with nesting boxes set on the shed shelves.

In this section we will go over the elements you need to include in a chicken coop. There are many creative ways to make sure all of these elements are incorporated within a simply designed, inexpensive coop. It is also possible to buy and find designs for chicken coops on the Internet, and even to buy pre-fabricated chicken coop kits that can be shipped to your home. Make sure any design you buy or use includes all of these elements and functions for your hens. One online source for pre-fabricated chicken coops are chickencoopsource.com and another is mypetchicken.com.

Photograph 10.11 Example of a Coop- Courtesy of Susie Biggs

Entrance

Obviously, your chickens need a way to enter their coop! The design of the entrance depends on the need for nighttime security from local predators. Off-the-ground entrances require a ladder you can remove at night to protect from predators. If your coop is on the ground, and you are concerned about predators, include a door that closes securely at night.

Egg Gathering and Cleaning Door

You will also need a way to retrieve the eggs and access the inside of the coop to clean out dirty bedding. For the greatest ease of maintenance, include a full-sized door that will allow you to walk into the coop. You may create two doors, one for cleaning, and one for gathering eggs. In some cases, the door for the chickens to enter their coop, and for you to enter the coop for cleaning and egg removal can all be the same door. It depends on how your coop is built.

Photograph 10.12a Egg Collecting Door - Closed

Photograph 10.12b Egg Collecting Door - Open

Roost

Chickens like to roost off the ground for sleeping. They feel and actually are safer clutching a branch or a piece of wood than they are on the ground. The roost doesn't have to be fancy. At Mother Nature Gardens, we stuck a stick in two holes in the wood planks inside our coop. The roost should be a 1- to 2-inch round dowel or stick, to make it easy for the hens to grasp with their claws. If you start with a square piece of wood, make sure to round the edges.

Photograph 10.13 Example of a Roost with a Hen on It

The Laying Box

A hen will lay eggs with or without a silk pillow to sit upon. In a pinch, she'll fashion a nest on the ground. If at all possible, however, encourage your hens to lay in the absolutely most convenient spot for you to gather the eggs. If you make a laying box and your hen or hens still choose the ground, entice them into the laying box by placing an egg in the box (real or plastic).

A laying box requires a minimum of three sides, creating about 12 square inches of space. Make the entrance side lower so your hens can easily find and enter the nest. Old dresser drawers make great laying boxes. Fill each box with a soft bed of straw and ideally provide one laying box for every three birds.

Photograph 10.14 Example of a Laying Box

Lighting and Heating

A hen needs 12 to 14 hours of sunlight a day in order to lay eggs. When the days are shorter, you can extend your laying season by adding a 25- to 40-watt bulb in the coop on a timer. Set the timer to come on for a couple hours after dusk and a couple hours before dawn. Some people feel that it is more natural to let the hens rest during the winter rather than encouraging them to lay year-round. This is up to you.

Chickens can tolerate very cold weather but they do not like drafts. Insulate your coop as the nights get colder by lining it with strawbales. If temperatures remain below 12 degrees at night, use the same 25- to 40-watt bulb and timer to heat the coop. Set the timer to come on several hours before dawn, the coldest hours of the day. You also can use a very small and safe heater in the coop that will turn off if it is tipped over. Electric or oil heaters may overheat the coop, however, so be careful and test your setup to make sure it is safe for your hens.

 ## The Run

Runs must be 6 to 8 square feet per bird. Hens need to be able to scratch in the dirt and dust themselves (their method of showering and cooling off in the summer heat, as well as keeping themselves free of insects). Rock and cement floors do not make good runs because the hens cannot scratch in them and take dust baths. If you have bare dirt in your run, lay fresh straw down regularly to give your hens something to scratch in. It makes them very happy to explore in the straw and break it down into dirt. If you don't have bare dirt to begin with, but have plants growing inside your run, the dirt will be bare after the chickens get a chance to spend some time in the run.

Hens need shade from the afternoon sun in the summer, *so the orientation of the coop and run is important.* You will need some kind of shade structure in the west that blocks the western sun. Be wary of having an unshaded run on the west side of your coop – it is likely to get too hot! As mentioned earlier, one option is to build the coop west of the run so that the coop itself shades the run.

It is helpful if you can arrange for the hens to have some outdoor space that is sheltered by a shade umbrella or overhang. This allows them to be outside their coop during the rain or snow.

You can keep the hens' watering supply in the run. However, you may wish to keep their feeder in a sheltered area so that the feed doesn't become soggy in the rain or snow.

The sides of the run can be made from many types of fencing materials and should be a good 6 feet tall to keep the birds from flying out, unless their wings are clipped, which we will discuss later in this chapter. Some runs include a covering over the top to ensure that birds stay inside and to further protect against predators, especially hawks and other raptors. It is also important to make sure that the way the fencing goes into the ground prevents dogs, cats, coyotes, and other predators from being able to enter under the fencing. At Mother Nature Gardens, we found we needed to bury the fencing and line it with rocks to keep animals (namely our dog hoping to share the kitchen scraps) from crawling underneath. Some people run the fencing down several inches into the ground, or down slightly, and then out a bit, buried, to discourage animals from digging their way under the fencing and into the run.

Photograph 10.15 Example of Chicken Runs-Melanie's Coop

Clipping the Hens' Wings

An alternative way to keep your hens from flying out of the run is to clip their wing feathers. This does not hurt them at all if you do it correctly. To clip wings, grab your chicken, sit down, and lay her gently on your lap. While one wing is pressed against your lap, spread the other one out. Identify the primary feathers, which are the longest ones, and cut two-thirds down the top of the feather. This will feel to the hen like nail cutting feels to us – in other words, it won't hurt. Do the other side. That should keep the hen from flying until she grows new feathers, which happens approximately once a year. If you are lucky, by the time the feathers grow back, your hens may have forgotten they can fly, and be content to stay on the ground.

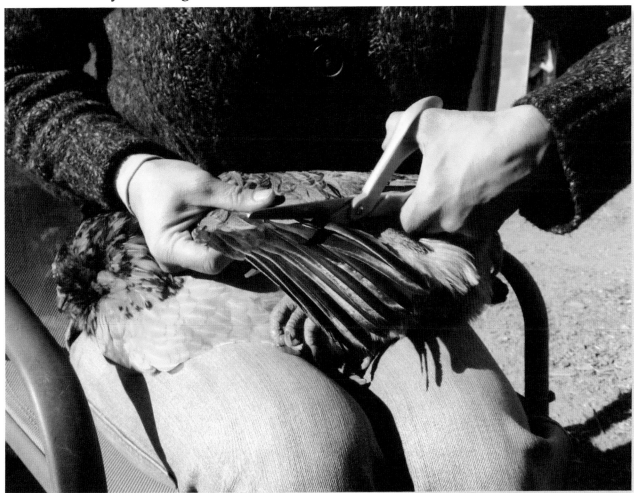

Photograph 10.16 Clipping a Hen's Wings

Our Home Farms
From Melanie

I built my coop as a demonstration for a class Zoe and I were holding on raising urban chickens. Along with Gretchen Beaubier and Will Becktell, who were part of a group of home farmers I worked with for a couple of years, (and many thanks to both of them for all their help!) I looked at coop designs and books to come up with the design. I decided I wanted to be able to walk into my coop to clean it and harvest the eggs. With my work schedule, I knew that if it wasn't easy to do these things, my hens would get less attention, and my eggs wouldn't be harvested as regularly. I wanted to make it very easy on myself.

I also wanted the coop to be cute when I and my neighbors viewed it from our houses. And I wanted it to have a barn theme.

The three of us built the coop first with a slanted corrugated roof and a little window, then added a run to the west. During the first summer we shaded this run with old patio umbrellas and this worked moderately well, but not really well enough. During the first winter I added an internal wall and door in the coop so that the hens could stay warm, and I also added a light on a timer inside, and during the coldest part of the winter, a small heater.

During the second summer I added another run on the eastern side of the coop, with a small door from the coop into this eastern run. The hens loved this second run in the afternoon because it was shaded by both the coop and a tree. (see Photograph 10.15 earlier in this chapter.)

This evolving process shows that you may not think of everything when you first build your coop, but in most situations you can adapt your design to make it work better over time as you learn more about your own and your hens' needs.

Photograph 10.17 Melanie's Coop

Harvesting Chickens

Of course, not all home farmers will want to harvest their chickens for meat. But for those who do, it is important to consider the possibility of harvesting your own meat because when you do it yourself, the process is typically far more humane than when you purchase chicken meat that came from a factory farm. When chickens are raised in large agribusiness, their cold, mechanical death can seem a relief from their tragic quality of life. Home-raised and butchered chicken is also much less expensive than buying ethically-raised and butchered chicken meat. Nothing gives us more respect and gratitude for life than death. With the proper equipment, a calm and centered demeanor, and a commitment to swift action, chicken butchering can cause very little suffering for the chicken.

Young chickens are the tastiest to harvest. Farmers raise fast-growing, meat-rich breeds, termed fryer chickens, from chicks and harvest them after about six months. Ask your local feed co-op what's available, or you can order these on line. Alternately, farmers will raise chicks for both eggs and meat and cull the flock of all the roosters soon after they reach maturity. At Mother Nature Gardens, we have harvested chickens for meat after their egg-producing begins to wane, at about four years. These birds produce tough meat that is best eaten in slowly cooked soups. If you wait too long to harvest a chicken, after five or six years, she can be nearly inedible. Some egg farmers will harvest chicken meat in the fall if they do not want to feed their slow egg producing flock over the winter.

To harvest a bird humanely, the minimum you need is a very sharp knife and a big pot of boiling water. The knife's sharpness is really quite important because it means the difference between a quick, clean cut at the chicken's neck and an insufferable sawing. A couple of other tools will aid the process. Harvesting cones can be purchased online or, if you are innovative and willing to do a little research, you can make them yourself. Before harvesting, you slip the chicken into the wide end of the cone and pull its head through the small opening on the other end. This holds the chicken still and exposes its neck while you make the terminal cut. Some people use large, sharp tree branch loppers to remove the head when using a cone. These cones are particularly handy if you are harvesting a number of birds. When I harvest, I simply hold the chicken between my legs and pull to extend its neck for the same result.

Photograph 10.18 Chicken Harvesting Cone

An additional tool I use for harvesting, following the local lore a neighbor told me about, is a needleless syringe filled with hard alcohol – vodka, whiskey (save your good stuff), or whatever is available. I catch my desired bird in the slowest, calmest manner possible. It is really important to be centered and present for this entire process. Like all animals, chickens perceive and respond to the emotions of the humans around them. If you are anxious and fearful, they will also become anxious and fearful and this will affect the quality of both their death and their meat. Also, if they get chased a great deal before being caught, adrenaline in their blood will toughen the meat. So it's good to get a meat bird used to being handled long before the harvest day. Once the bird is caught, I open its beak and inject my prepared syringe of alcohol down its throat. A little toddy has the same effect on the bird that it does on us; it relaxes the bird and reduces pain sensation. I sit with the bird for several minutes then, allowing the alcohol to take effect and giving both the bird and myself time to relax after the catch.

Then, stick the bird in the killing cone or, if not using a cone, clamp the bird, wing against its body, between your legs. Pull the neck out tight. You will aim for the top, inside of the neck, just below its jawline. This is where the main artery is located. You may want to pluck the feathers away from its neck where you will make the cut so the knife enters with greater ease. Give thanks and make a forceful cut following the angle of the jaw-line. You may need more than one cut to assure you have severed the jugular. Half-assed, fear-shaky cuts create suffering. Commit to the process and then give it all you've got. The chicken will die and be out of pain within seconds after its jugular vein is cut, but it takes a while for all the life to move out of its body. The wings will flap and it will even run if you let it go, thus the saying "Running around like a chicken with its head cut off." I usually hold the chicken upside down by its feet until all movement stops. Then hang the chicken in this position for a while to let the blood drain from its neck into a bucket or other appropriate receptacle.

Once the emotionally-challenging part of harvesting is over, the next step is the laborious part of chicken harvesting, which is cleaning the bird. After the blood stops draining (10 minutes), dunk the bird into a prepared pot of boiling or near-boiling water for about 60 seconds. This will make plucking very easy. Pull the bird out and begin extracting feathers in the direction opposite to the way the feathers lie, and be careful not to burn yourself (you may want to wear rubber gloves for protection). Add the feathers to your worm bin or compost pile. Cut off the bird's feet (these make delightful treats for curious canines on the farm).

Now, make a shallow cut from the bird's anus to the top of its breast. Ideally, you will not puncture its intestines or its stomach, or a pungent odor will make the job uncomfortable. Cutting through the breastbone takes a bit of muscle. Then, cut around the anus so you pull out the entire internal cavity in one piece. Use your knife to cut the membranes that hold the organs to the skeleton. I bury the internal organs in my yard, including the liver and heart, which other more adventurous cooks keep. Rinse the bird thoroughly and refrigerate or freeze immediately. You are now ready for a truly farm-fresh dinner. *Bon appetit!*

 Exercise 10.1 Planning Your Chicken Adventure

Take a few minutes and think about your own plans for raising chickens:

1. Are you ready to raise chickens? Why or why not?

2. Does your property have an appropriate space for raising chickens?

3. Are your family members or housemates on board with raising chickens? What about your neighbors? What communications would smooth the way for this endeavor?

4. Will you raise your hens free-range, in a chicken tractor, or in a stationary coop?

5. How many will you get and what type? Will you buy them as pullets or as chicks?

6. If you are building a coop, where will you locate it? How accessible is this to your kitchen?

7. How will you go about designing your coop? How much money do you have to spend on your coop? What materials will you use?

8. What help will you need with the design and building, and who can help you?

Chapter Eleven:
Introduction to Raising Honeybees

By Melanie Rubin with Dr. Gary Moses

Overview

If this is the first time you've thought about raising honey bees, welcome to this exciting endeavor! The first time I saw the inside of a hive, I fell in love with honeybees and their mystery. For me, a beehive holds a special energy that I find deeply soothing, nourishing, and relaxing. I hope you share that experience with me! Standing by a hive and watching the bees fly in and out always makes me happy.

This chapter will provide you with enough of an introduction to help you decide if you want to keep bees and to get you started. It will *not* give you a complete and comprehensive explanation of everything you could possibly need to know to raise honeybees, but it is a start. You can broaden your bee knowledge by reading any of the wonderful bee books already written. My experience has shown me that in addition to book learning, becoming a good beekeeper requires a good mentor – someone with whom you can experience beekeeping and discuss the questions or issues that arise when the hive is open. As a start, find the opportunity, as soon as you can, to be a guest when a beekeeper tends one of his or her hives. This will help you decide whether raising honeybees is for you. You might check out, for example, whether there is a local beekeeping club or association, and contact them to find out whether they know of classes, or opportunities to visit with a local beekeeper.

Personally, I am new to beekeeping. My first introduction to bees was when an accomplished top bar beekeeper named Casey Paul taught a class in my backyard as part of the Albuquerque Backyard Farms workshop series we were running that summer. Casey brought over a top bar hive one Sunday evening, a few days before the workshop, and I lived with them in my yard for about a week. I found their presence magical and deliciously sweet, like honey.

In the spring of 2010, I had the opportunity to study beekeeping with Alison Yahna, an accomplished beekeeper on the Big Island of Hawaii. Alison's work falls into the ancient tradition of shamanic beekeeping, which taps into what many people feel is the deep spirituality and wisdom of the honeybees. Living and working with Alison for a week was truly amazing, and I was hooked.

Returning to the mainland, I began studying with Dr. Gary Moses, who is my naturopathic physician. He is also a third generation beekeeper who is a master in all aspects of beekeeping working with Langstroth hives (something I'll explain soon), and has a small commercial company in Albuquerque, NM. Dr. Moses and I began going out on Sunday afternoons to tend his bees, and I started to learn more about how to work with the bees in a hands-on, practical way. Dr. Moses helped me set up my first hive in June 2010, and I began to tend bees on my own.

I am continuing to learn under Dr. Moses' tutelage as a new and fascinated beekeeper. I hope you will enjoy this learning process as much as I do.

Dr. Moses has generously agreed to co-author this chapter on beekeeping. I am more grateful than I can say for his help and support.

Why Keep Bees?

Most people become beekeepers first and foremost because they are fascinated by the bees and love working with them. It is a glorious and special privilege to be part of the inner workings of a hive, even for a moment. Of course, the products of the hive are wonderful – honey, pollen, propolis, and wax. We will talk about each of these in this chapter. And many people keep bees to help pollinate the plants in their garden.

It is becoming more and more important for backyard beekeepers to have honeybee hives. In many parts of the world, a phenomenon known as colony collapse has become prevalent, where bees suddenly abandon their hives, or die in the hive. There are many explanations for this tragedy, including global warming, habitat loss, the increasing concentration of pesticides in honeybee hives, commercial queen rearing and beekeeping practices that may weaken the bees, appearance of mites and other pests that kill the bees, and some more esoteric (and to my way of thinking powerful and plausible) explanations of why the honeybees may be inclined to abandon their millennia-old collaboration with humans. Whatever the cause, the number of hives in the United States is now at the lowest that it has been in 50 years, and researchers estimate that nearly one-third of all honeybee colonies in the United States has vanished.

Regardless of why hive collapse is happening, it seems to many people imperative to do whatever we can to maintain and support the honeybee population. Honeybees play a major role in our food supply, pollinating at least 30% of the world's crops. The following quote has been attributed to Einstein:

"If the bee disappears from the surface of the earth, man would have no more than four years to live."

Backyard beekeeping is important because it helps to create a diversity of honeybee populations that can cross breed and remain strong and resilient. It is a grassroots way to help restore honeybees and beekeeping to a balanced, healthy state, through lots of little efforts that counter some of the damaging effects of large, industrialized agriculture, in the same way that home farming can help to address some of the dangers of large-scale commercial farming. It also makes honeybees more visible within mainstream culture, and keeps people aware of the necessity of protecting the honeybees.

Of course, urban honeybees also help to pollinate urban and home farms. And when urban honeybees are well cared for, with swarm-prevention management techniques, and bred from gentle honeybee strains, municipalities see that urban honeybees are not a threat. Then, they become amenable to having honeybees in an urban environment, rather than passing regulations that prohibit the raising of urban honeybees.

To find out whether beekeeping is legal within your town or city, try Google-ing "Is beekeeping legal in ____(name of city, town, state)."

It is a good idea to speak with your neighbors before establishing a bee hive near their property line. And, it is best to locate your hive or hives in an area where your neighbors are unlikely to be frequenting, as well as to place the hive near a wall that will cause the bees to fly up above the neighbor's property as they exit the hive. If your neighbors have a concern about the hive, you may want to invite them to don a bee suit and visit the inside of the hive with you. Once they see how amazing the bees are, they are more likely to want to support beekeeping on your property. Offering them some honey can help, too! And explaining that most bees only sting when they are threatened is useful in allaying the fears of people who are afraid of bees. Of course, if your neighbors happen to be allergic to bee stings, this is a special situation that needs to be carefully taken into consideration.

Later in this chapter, we will talk about the benefits to the individual beekeeper of keeping honeybees, including bee stings for health purposes!

Safety

The first question people have about beekeeping is usually, "Is it dangerous? Will I get stung?" Of course, this question is most relevant if you happen to be allergic to bee stings – in which case, getting stung can cause an anaphylactic shock reaction. This type of allergy is prevalent in only 2% of the population, and can be addressed immediately with the use of epinephrine treatment in the form of a self-injectable EpiPen, which people who know they are allergic to bees tend to carry with them when they are outdoors.

Honeybees typically will only sting if they perceive that the hive is threatened. Only female bees (the majority of the bees) have stingers and they die when they lose their stingers, so as you can imagine, stinging for no reason is not high on their list of evolutionary behaviors.

Many beekeepers wear a full bee suit with hat and veil and gloves to protect themselves from being stung, and this makes beekeeping generally quite safe.

Photograph 11.1 Beekeeper Jessie Brown in a Full Beekeeping Suit
brownsdowntownbees.blogspot.com

Some beekeepers only wear a hat, veil, long sleeves, and gloves when working in the hive, and others generally feel quite safe with no protective equipment on at all. This is a personal choice. However, if you are performing a task that is likely to agitate the bees, it is best at least to wear some type of protective gear.

When a honeybee stings, she releases venom called apitoxin into the skin, along with attack pheremones that alert the other bees to the danger. If you are stung, to minimize the risk of being stung again by other bees, it is important to remove the stinger as quickly as possible. The best way to do this is to scrape the stinger horizontally off your skin with a fingernail, rather than trying to pull it out, which can actually drive the venom deeper into the skin. If you are stung, you can apply a topical solution of Benadryl, take Benadryl orally, and also take the homeopathic remedy Apis, which can be found at many natural foods stores. Zoe has had success with applying tobacco leaves at the sting point.

Honeybees will respond to the way you approach the hive. It is best to be calm and centered, move slowly, and wear white or light-colored clothing when working with honeybees.

History of Beekeeping

The history of humans raising honeybees dates back to almost 2500 BC in Egypt. There is evidence of apiculture in prehistoric Greece, and in Israel dating back 3,000 years, as well as in ancient China. For example, Aristotle was a beekeeper. The word "medicine" was originally "melacine" from the word "mela," which means honey in Greek. And at first, the caduceus symbol of medicine, which shows two snakes around a winged staff, was originally actually a jar of honey, with the honey streaming down the staff, which was later interpreted as a serpent. Hippocrates, who is considered to be the father of Western medicine, used honey as an ingredient in many remedies. Bee products including, of course, honey, as well as propolis, pollen, and beeswax, have been used throughout recorded history as food, medicine, cosmetics, and even as secret ingredients in all sorts of products, including in the lacquer used to seal Stradivari's famous violins in the 17th and 18th centuries.

 ## The Skep Hive

The first type of manmade bee hive was the Skep hive, an inverted, woven basket made out of wicker plastered with mud or dung, or made of coils of grass or straw. Two disadvantages of this type of hive were that beekeepers could not inspect the hives for diseases and pests, and honey removal was not easy, often resulting in the destruction of the entire colony.

Drawing 11.1 Drawing of Traditional Skep Hives

 The Top Bar Hive or Kenyan Hive

The top bar hive originated in Africa, and is also known as the Kenyan hive. The earliest top bar hives are believed to be thousands of years old and were baskets with sticks laid across the top as bars. These hives allowed the beekeepers to harvest only the honey that was ripe, without destroying any bees in the hive. The Kenyan hives have sloped sides and the Tanzanian hives have vertical sides.

In a top bar hive, a long hive box has bars laid across the top and the bees build their comb vertically from these bars. A typical Kenyan-style top bar hive might have 30 removable bars. The bees tend to build and fill the comb from the front to the back, with brood (bee eggs and larvae) closest to the entrance, and then pollen, and then honey farthest from the entrance to the hive. This mirrors how honeybees build a hive in nature.

Photograph 11.2 A Series of Topbar Hives. brownsdowntownbees.blogspot.com

Top bar hives are simple and inexpensive to build. They have the advantage of making it easy to see everything that is happening in the hive by lifting one bar at a time, whereas Langstroth hives require opening various layers of boxes if you want to examine what is going on throughout the hive. Top bar hives also require less equipment for processing the honey, since you can cut the honeycomb and use it as is, or squeeze it manually to extract the honey. Some people say that top bar hives also create an environment that is more natural and healthy for the bees, because the bees create and regulate the size of their honeycomb cells themselves.

A disadvantage of top bar hives is that they require more frequent maintenance to check whether the bees have run out of room. Once the bars in a top bar hive are full of comb, and the comb is full, the beekeeper must replace the full bars with empty bars, otherwise the bees may be inclined to swarm to find new, roomier quarters. With Langstroth hives, by contrast, the beekeeper can always add a new box within the hive structure, called a super, to create more room for the bees to work. This allows more bees to live in the hive, and to produce more honey within their single hive. Many commercial beekeepers say that top bar hives are more difficult to use for commercial beekeeping operations because extraction of honey does not lend itself well to mechanization and is therefore too time consuming and labor intensive. In top bar hives, the bees also may be inclined to attach wax between the bars or to the walls of the hive, and to cement the frames to the side of the box creating what is called "burr comb." This tendency can make it difficult to extract the bars and comb without disturbing significant portions of the hive. Also, a top bar hive takes up more horizontal space than a Langstroth hive, so a top bar hive can be disadvantageous if space is limited, such as in a home farming environment.

The Langstroth Hive

In 1851, the Reverend Lorenzo Lorraine Langstroth of Philadelphia discovered that if a space of ⅜ of an inch is left in the hive for the bees to move around in, the bees will not build comb in the space or cement it shut. He called this the "bee space." Ultimately he used this idea in the design of a hive frame that discouraged the bees from attaching honeycomb to the inside of the hive box. Subsequent inventions by Jan Dzierzon and others helped to further develop this idea.

In modern day Langstroth hives, the frames have a flat sheet of foundation inserted into them, which is made out of wax or plastic and, imprinted with a honeycomb cell pattern. The bees then build their honeycomb on top of this pattern, making their cells the size of the imprinted cells in the foundation. Foundation can be purchased with slightly different cell sizes.

Typically there are eight to 10 frames in a Langstroth hive box, depending on how deeply the beekeeper wants the bees to draw out the cells, and whether the beekeeper also needs to include a feeder in the box. When a feeder needs to be included in place of a frame and/or when the beekeeper wants to encourage the bees to draw out their cells more deeply, fewer frames are included in the hive. (Sometimes it is appropriate to feed the bees with a mixture of cane sugar and water. We will discuss this more below.)

Photograph 11.3 Langstroth Hive- Courtesy of Alison Yahna, artemissmiles.com

Helpful Notes: Parts of a Langstroth Hive

The Langstroth bee hive includes the following elements, from top to bottom:

• A cover

• An inner cover

• One or more hive body boxes, made of wood or plastic, each with 8 to 10 frames of wood or plastic and a foundation made of wax on wire or plastic. The upper boxes are called "supers."

• An optional queen excluder divider (explained below).

• A bottom board

• An optional entrance reducer, which makes the entrance to the hive smaller for the bees to guard

The bees fill a Langstroth hive from the bottom to the top. The first frames, usually in the center of the bottom box, contain brood – the eggs the queen lays that will become larvae and ultimately new bees. The bees tend to put stores of honey and pollen for food in the outer frames. As they fill the bottom box, they move upward into the supers to continue their work. Often beekeepers will use supers that are half the height of the lower boxes, since these boxes become very heavy when they are filled with honeycomb. If a queen excluder is placed between the first or second box and subsequent higher boxes, then all of the brood will be maintained in the lower one or two boxes, and the top boxes will contain only honey and sometimes some pollen.

One advantage of the Langstroth hive system is that with the right equipment, which we will discuss later, it is easier to process the products of the hive in volume. Also, a full hive box can easily be removed and set aside for later processing, whereas with a top bar hive, it is more difficult to store full frames of honeycomb, so immediate processing is often necessary. Langstroth hives are also standardized in terms of size, design, and interchangeability. This allows beekeepers to buy, sell, share, and trade hive parts, optimizing the use of equipment. With Langstroth hives, equipment is available to collect pollen so that people can have pollen from their own neighborhood. This is beneficial as a food supplement and for desensitizing people to local allergens. Pollen is typically sold as granules and can be eaten on a spoon, mixed in with cereal, or sprinkled on other foods. Devices specifically for collecting pollen are not generally available for top bar hives.

One disadvantage of Langstroth hive structures is that they are less natural because the foundation in Langstroth hives provides a pattern that directs the size of the honeycomb cells the bees draw out from the foundation. Some beekeepers perceive this as an advantage, however, because the smaller comb cells limit the number of drones that are produced, so that more worker bees are produced, which then produce more honey. We will talk more later on in this chapter about the roles of worker bees, drones, and the queen in the hive. Langstroth beekeeping also requires more equipment to process the products of the hive. We will also talk later in this chapter about where to buy hive parts and what they cost.

The Bee Caste System and Functions – Understanding the Hive and Colony

 **Overview**

Honeybees are social insects that live in a group and die as individuals. They live in a caste system that includes three tiers: workers, drones, and the queen.

 The Worker Bee

The worker bee is the backbone of the hive, makes up the majority of its residents, and performs most of the functions in the hive besides reproducing. Worker bees are non-fertile females and are the smallest bees in the hive. From 2,000 to 60,000 worker bees live in a healthy bee colony. Worker bees perform these different tasks at the three different stages in their life cycle, which include brood, house bee, and field bee.

- Cleaning cell walls
- Tending the queen
- Feeding incubating larvae
- Building comb
- Circulating air
- Processing nectar
- Packing pollen
- Patrolling and guarding the hive
- Foraging for nectar and pollen

Worker bees can live from four weeks to several months, depending on the time of year. During the middle of the summer when they can work up to 12 hours a day, worker bees typically live only about four weeks. During the winter when activity is low, the small number of worker bees that remain in the hive can live for months.

Worker bees require approximately three weeks to incubate, depending on weather and other conditions. The bee begins life as a fertilized egg that has been laid by the queen. After three days, the egg hatches into a larva. The larva is fed royal jelly and later, a mixture of honey and pollen, called bee bread, by worker bees that have taken on the role of nurse bees. Royal jelly is secreted from glands in the hypopharynx of the nurse bees. Each larva grows tremendously over the next three days. After six days, feeding stops, the cell is capped, and the larva becomes a pupa. After another 12 days or so, the pupa transforms into a full-sized worker bee, and ultimately hatches. The brood cells for worker bees (the cells where they incubate) are flat when they are capped and make up the majority of the brood in the hive.

Photograph 11.4 Capped Worker Brood. brownsdowntownbees.blogspot.com

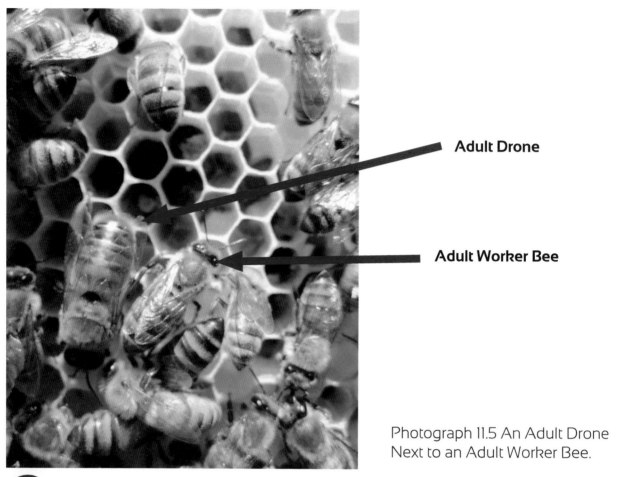

Adult Drone

Adult Worker Bee

Photograph 11.5 An Adult Drone Next to an Adult Worker Bee.

The Drone Bee

Drone bees are the males of the colony. Their only function is to mate with the queen or a queen from another hive. Their numbers vary from none in the winter to 500 during mating and swarm season. They are larger bees with big eyes that they use to locate the queen during her mating flight. They do not have stingers.

Drone bees develop from unfertilized eggs that are laid by the queen. They have half the number of chromosomes as the worker bees. The incubation cycle and feeding for a drone bee is similar to that of a worker bee, except that a drone bee spends 10 days as a larva before his cell is capped and he goes into the pupa phase. And drone bees hatch after approximately 24 days, as opposed to 21 for worker bees. Brood cells for drone bees have a rounded top when they are capped, allowing more room for the formation of a larger insect.

Drone Bee Brood

Queen Cup Cell

Photograph 11.6 Drone Bee Brood with Queen Cup. Cell After Queen has Hatched.
brownsdowntownbees.blogspot.com

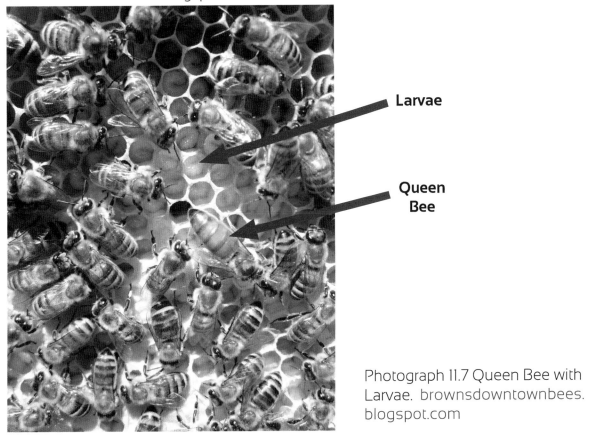

Larvae

Queen Bee

Photograph 11.7 Queen Bee with Larvae. brownsdowntownbees. blogspot.com

The Queen Bee

There is only one queen bee in each colony and she controls the mood, activity, and survival of the hive. She has a long abdomen, short wings, and a barbless stinger. The queen bee is usually found in the brood section of the hive.

Queen bees develop from fertilized eggs laid by a previous queen. If the old queen has left the hive, the worker bees will create a new queen, provided appropriate eggs are present. During incubation the queen bee spends three days as an egg, six days as a larva, and another eight days in a capped cell as a pupa, emerging after the 16th day. Queens are fed more heavily with royal jelly during the larva stage, and this is what causes them to incubate into a queen rather than into a worker bee. The brood cell for a queen has a tubular shape when it is fully formed and capped.

If the hive needs a new queen, the worker bees will create several queen cells. Once the new queens hatch, the most dominant queen will sting the others to death so that the hive only has one queen.

The newly-established queen typically makes one or more orientation flights out of the hive three to five days after she is born to practice her new flying skills and ensure that she can find her way back home. Then seven to 10 days after she is born, she goes on her mating flight, and mates with up to 20 drones. Often mating takes place in drone congregation areas, where drones from all the colonies in the neighborhood, including feral colonies, gather and wait for virgin queens to appear. This cross-breeding between hives keeps the hives from becoming inbred, and allows them to remain strong genetically.

A queen can lay up to 2,500 eggs in one day and can live for up to four years.

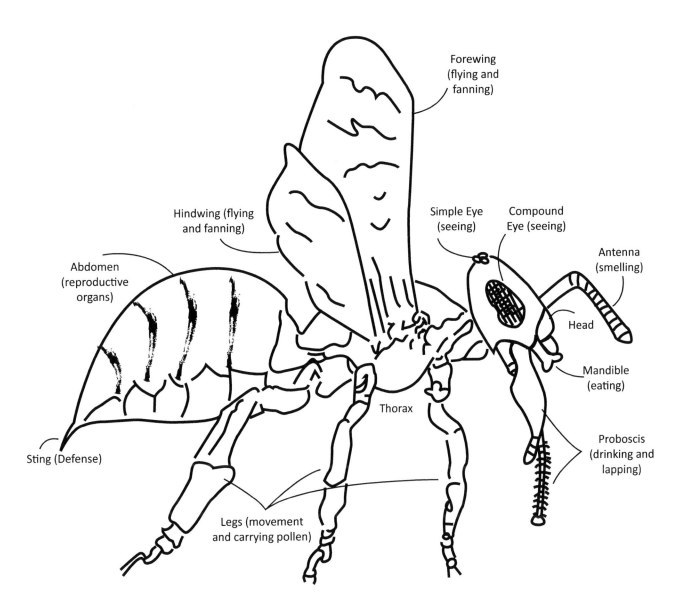

Drawing 11.2 Parts of a Female Honeybee

What You Can Harvest from the Hive

There are several possible products from the hive. They have many uses, and can all be sold.

Honey and Honey Comb

Honey is the number one product from the hive. Along with pollen, it is the bees' food. It is delicious for humans, and full of healthy enzymes and nutrients. Honey is made from flower nectar that has been distilled into a solution that is less than 20% water. Eating local honey can help people with allergies be more resistant to local pollens. Honey is also excellent for treating burns. And many people enjoy eating honeycomb, which is honey that is still in the wax cells in which the bees created it.

Photograph 11.8 Honeybees with Capped and Uncapped Honey - Courtesy of Alison Yahna
artemissmiles.com

Pollen

Pollen is the honeybees' source of protein. It can be harvested from the hive and eaten by humans as well, as a tasty and healthy treat. Eating local pollen, like eating local honey, can help prevent seasonal allergies.

 # Wax

Beeswax is the housing for honeybees. They produce and manipulate it into hexagonal cells that hold their honey, pollen, and brood. Beeswax can be used to make candles and salves.

 # Propolis

Bees make propolis from the resin in tree buds and sap flows and use it as a sealant for small unwanted spaces in the hive; for example, to reduce the size of the opening to the hive. It has very strong antimicrobial properties and is used in tinctures as an immune system builder. Propolis tincture works very effectively when taken at the first sign of a cold. Within the hive, propolis looks like a greenish or brownish gummy resin.

 # Royal Jelly

Worker bees produce royal jelly from a gland in the head and use it to feed the brood. It is full of vitamins and other nutrients, and can be eaten by humans. Royal jelly is believed to have certain health benefits, such as lowering cholesterol, combating unhelpful bacteria, healing wounds, boosting the immune system, promoting the growth of neural cells, and calming inflammation.

In the following section we will cover the tools for getting started with beekeeping, and will address, in part, the procedures for harvesting these products. For a more complete description of harvesting procedures, we recommend the book *The Backyard Beekeeper's Honey Handbook* by Kim Flottum.

How to Get Started, Including the Tools for Beekeeping

 ## Overview of Tools and Where to Buy Them

The tools and equipment you will need to begin beekeeping fall into several categories:

- Hive parts
- Hive tools
- Protection gear
- Harvesting equipment

As we've discussed earlier, it's a little bit less expensive to get started with top bar beekeeping because you need less hive and harvesting equipment. It is also possible to build a top bar hive yourself. If you are interested in doing that, you may want to search the Internet for a top bar hive design; many are available for free. You can build many if not all of the hive components for Langstroth beekeeping as well – it just depends on how handy you are.

Many suppliers are available from whom you can buy the tools and equipment you need for beekeeping. One of the most well-known is Dadant & Sons, Inc. (dadant.com). Another supplier is backyardhive.com, which sells top bar equipment. To save money, you may also want to look for used equipment through a local beekeeping association, by contacting local beekeepers, or by advertising on Craigslist and other used equipment shopping services and web sites.

The estimated costs provided below are for new equipment, except where indicated.

Top Bar Hive Beekeeping

1. *Hive*

You will need the actual hive itself. This can be free if you can build it yourself, or can cost up to approximately $200 or more if you purchase a hive, depending on how fancy it is. For example, a colleague in New Mexico built an amazing top bar hive that looked like a modern Asian pagoda and had a viewing window to watch the bees at work – the materials for that hive probably cost a couple hundred dollars.

2. *Foundation Strips and Beeswax*

You may wish to purchase some wax foundation and beeswax to install on the top bars. You will need to cut strips of foundation about two inches wide to adhere to the length of the top bar with melted beeswax. You can melt the beeswax in a can on the top of your stove, and use an old paintbrush to adhere the foundation strips to the top bars with the melted wax. This could cost you from $11 to $30.

Langstroth Hive Beekeeping

1. *Hive*

You will need two hive boxes for brood, plus one or more super boxes, an inner cover, top cover, and bottom board. You can often buy starter kits that include all of these supplies. The cost for a kit like this can range from $110 to $300.

2. *Foundation for Frames*

This will cost you $12 to $50, depending on whether you use beeswax foundation or plastic foundation. (Beeswax is more expensive.)

3. *Queen Excluder*

This piece of equipment prevents the queen bee from going into the upper boxes in a Langstroth hive. It makes sure the upper boxes only contain honey and possibly pollen rather than brood, which is desirable for separating out the products you will harvest from the hive. The cost is $5 to $15.

4. Frame Holder

This piece of equipment allows you to hold a frame on the side of the hive while you are working in the hive. Cost is approximately $25.

5. Frame Grip Tool

This tool allows you to pick up a frame easily from inside the hive. Cost is $11 to $20.

6. Extractor

This machine uses centrifugal force to extract honey from the frames. It is the most expensive piece of equipment you will buy for Langstroth beekeeping that you will not need for top bar beekeeping. The cost for an extractor can range from $120 for a small, hobby, plastic version, to $1,300 – or you can build your own.

Tools and Equipment for Working with Either Kind of Hive

1. Smoker

For smoking the hive when you open it, to calm the bees, and warn them that you are coming in. Cost is approximately $30 to $50

2. Hive Tool or Knife

For prying open the hive, and moving frames or bars around within the hive. Cost is approximately $5.

3. Veil

For covering your head, face, and neck. Cost is approximately $11 to $20.

4. Helmut or Hat

To wear with your veil. This can be a specialized item, or whatever you have that has a sturdy brim. Cost is approximately $11 to $20.

5. Gloves for Working with Bee Equipment

Long-sleeved gloves cost approximately $11 to $20.

6. Glass Jars for Bottling Honey

7. Smoker Fuel

You can gather this – it will include something like newspaper that lights quickly, and dried lavender or sage, some sticks, and other slower-burning materials.

Recommended Tools and Equipment

1. Stainless Steel Double Sieve

   This is a pan that is used to strain honey. The cost is approximately $50

2. Pallet or cinder blocks for raising your hive off the ground.

3. A brush for brushing bees off of frames or bars. Cost is approximately $3 to $5

4. A tool for scratching the caps off the tops of capped cells of honey. Cost is approximately $5 to $11

5. Device for reducing the size of the hive entrance. Cost is approximately $1 to $3

6. Entrance feeder, and/or division board feeder. Each is approximately $5

7. Devices for feeding the bees, each approximately $5

8. Bee protection suit. Cost is approximately $50 to $75.

Other Tools You May Want

1. *Nuke Box*

   A nuke box is used for creating a split from the hive and starting a new hive. It is beyond the scope of this chapter to cover the procedure for making a split, but you can read about it in the references we have included in this chapter. The cost is approximately $20 to $50.

2. *Solar Wax Melter*

   For melting, using, and reusing beeswax. You can make your own or buy one for $60 on up.

3. *Pollen Trap*

   This is used for catching pollen in the hive so that you can use it as a product. The cost is approximately $35 to $55.

 **Where to Get Your Bees**

Overview

There are three options for getting bees to start a hive: purchasing all your bees; purchasing or receiving a nuke hive; or catching or receiving a swarm.

Option One: Purchase all your bees

You can purchase bees through a supplier. This option works for both top bar and Langstroth hives. It is best to purchase bees early in the season before they run out. One supplier is R Weaver Company in Texas, rweaver.com. Three pounds of bees including a queen will cost you about $90.

Option Two: Purchase a nuke hive

This option only works for a Langstroth hive, as the frames in a nuke box are designed to go into a Langstroth hive. You can purchase a nuke hive from a local beekeeper. For example, in New Mexico, Dr. Moses sells nuke hives with nuke box return to him for $70, or if you keep the box, the total cost is $95.

Option Three: Catch a swarm

This option works for both top bar and Langstroth hives. If you are fortunate enough to locate a swarm, you can (with a bee suit on!) place a cardboard box under the swarm, preferably at night, smoke the bees, and then snip the branch the swarm is on so that the whole swarm drops into the box. You can then "pour" the bees into the hive. You can also try contacting a local bee association to find out whether there are any people doing swarm relocation who would be willing to give or sell you a swarm.

Photograph11.9 Bee Swarm. brownsdowntownbees.blogspot.com

Locating Your Hive

Here are a few tips for locating your hive in your yard or on your property:

- Talk to your neighbors about where you will locate the bees and, if possible, place the bees in a location that is near the back of both of your properties so they are away from heavily trafficked areas.

- Ideally, pick a location that faces eastward and has afternoon shade.

- Make a water source available to the bees that includes a place for them to land and drink without drowning. A water basin with rocks in it works well. A water feeder for chickens also works well.

- Plan your garden plantings to benefit your bees.

What to Plant in Your Yard to Benefit Honeybees

Bees need plants that flower and produce both pollen and nectar throughout the spring, summer, and fall. Some weeds, for example, are highly beneficial to bees because they are early sources of food, like dandelions and mustard greens. Consider letting your weeds flower, and then cutting them down before they go to seed.

Note that one of the ways you can be supportive of honeybees in our ecosystem, even if you don't want to raise bees, is by growing bee-friendly plants in your garden.

Beneficial plants for bees include:

- Sunflowers (which are very important for many things in your garden)
- Russian sage
- Lavender
- Rosemary
- Marjoram
- Basil, if you let it flower

- Any wild flower mix
- Fruit trees
- Garden vegetables that flower, such as legumes and plants from the nightshade family
- Oregon grape
- Hyssop
- Bee balm
- Nepeta (Cat mint)

For more ideas on plants that are beneficial to bees, see the book *American Honey Plants* by Frank C. Pellett, copyright 1920 and published by Dadant & Sons. Many editions of this book have been published and it is often available at used book stores. You also might search the Internet for a copy.

Maintenance for Your Hive

Here are a few things to consider in maintaining your hive:

- Especially in the early spring, it is important to feed your bees before a lot of nectar and pollen is available if it seems like they may have run out of food.

- At all times of the year, make sure water is available to your bees, with a place for them to land and drink without drowning.

- During the spring, summer, and fall, check the hive regularly to make sure there is enough free space in the hive for the bees to create new cells, for the queen to lay eggs, and for the storing of pollen and honey.

- During the spring, summer, and fall, also check to make sure there is brood in the hive. If there is not brood, the hive has lost the queen, and you may need to re-queen the hive.

- Check for signs of illnesses and pests. These may include:
  - American foul brood
  - European foul brood

- Sac brood (chalkbrood)

- Damage to the bees from insecticide

- Varoa mites

- Tracheal mites (Nosema)

Because this is such a big topic, if it seems like your hive is weakened, or the bees are ill, contact an experienced beekeeper for advice, or the state bee inspector by calling the county agent of the local extension service. One book that has good information about natural ways for dealing with pests and diseases is *Natural Beekeeping* by Ross Conrad.

In Langstroth hives, also check to make sure the frames are in good working order, and replace or repair any frames that are beginning to come apart. When necessary, replace foundation in the frames.

- In the fall, make sure to leave enough honey in the hive to carry the bees through the winter. A top bar hive typically requires 12 bars of honey to get through a winter. The colder and longer the winter, the more honey the bees will need. For example, in the south where it's warm, a beekeeper might leave only one hive box for the bees to overwinter within. Whereas in the north, where the winters are longer, the bees will need at least one super full of honey and perhaps two to overwinter. It is also helpful to be able to check on the bees during a warm, sunny day during the winter, to make sure the bees have enough food. If their food supply seems to be slim, the beekeeper can feed the bees with a cane sugar and water mixture, or place a frame or two of honey inside the hive. Some beekeepers just put granulated sugar on top of the inner cover of the hive, where the bees can easily access it, without opening up the hive in the cold.

- Before the winter, winterize your hive by placing an extra layer of insulation or an insulating top on the hive. Ensure that the hive is in a place that is protected from cold winds and preferably has some coverage against snow.

If you only have one hive, you can count on spending, on average, a couple of hours a month attending to your bees and your hive, maintaining them, and processing the products of the hive.

Processing Your Bee Products

 ## Harvesting Honey

You can begin harvesting honey from the hive in midsummer if and when it is clear that the bees have enough reserves for themselves. This is easy to do in a Langstroth hive, because it only requires you to remove the full honey supers and replace them with empty boxes. In a top bar hive, you would remove the extra bars that have comb, which is full of capped honey.

For both Langstroth and top bar hives, the next step is to scratch the cappings off the cells that hold the honey. With top bar comb, you will then manually squeeze the honey out of the cells and press the mash through a high quality screen into a holding pot. You can then cover the screen with a large cloth and let the honey drain for a day. With Langstroth frames, you will put the frames in an extractor and spin the frames to extract the honey before straining the honey using a double sieve strainer of some type.

Then package the honey by pouring it into sterilized, dried glass jars. Make sure not to get any water in the jars, as this might cause the honey to ferment.

 ## Harvesting Honey Comb

In a top bar hive, you can cut honeycomb directly from the bars of honey and package them in plastic bags or glass jars. In a Langstroth hive, you can buy and use special frames that make it easy to remove and package sections of honey comb.

 ## Harvesting Pollen

You can buy pollen traps that either fit onto the front of the hive or slide underneath it. When worker bees crawl through the screen in a pollen trap, any pollen that has been stored on their legs is knocked off into the pollen trap. There is a drawer in the pollen trap that you can slide out to empty it.

Next, put the pollen in the freezer to kill any moth larvae that may be in it. Then dry it by putting the trays of pollen in a food dehydrator. Finally, you will need to put it through a pollen cleaner (another item you can buy or make) to blow out any bee parts that may have gotten mixed into the pollen. To get an idea of what this device might look like, visit kelleybees.com and search "pollen cleaner." At this point you can package it for use or sale.

 ## Harvesting Propolis

To harvest propolis, you will need to have a solar wax melter. The melter separates the propolis from the beeswax because the propolis has a much higher melting point and is heavier than beeswax. Once the beeswax has drained off, you can collect the propolis. Or, if the solar melter has gotten hot enough to melt them both, the propolis will settle to the bottom of the wax, and can be scraped off the bottom once the beeswax has cooled. The propolis is a dark brown color, whereas beeswax is yellow.

The propolis that has been heated in a solar wax melter is sterile, i.e. it doesn't have bacteria in it. It may still contain other impurities, however, such as dirt or bee parts. Most of the propolis that is sold commercially has been extracted with alcohol to remove these impurities. It is mixed with 190- to 200-proof grain alcohol, which dissolves it. After it is dissolved, it can be poured through a filter (coffee filters work well). The propolis will go through the filter, and any impurities will get caught on the filter.

The remaining alcohol/propolis mixture can be put in dropper bottles and used orally or externally as an antiseptic or antioxidant. The main benefit of propolis is the polyphenols it contains, which are very powerful antioxidants. The propolis/alcohol tincture can also be mixed with other ingredients to create various types of health products and remedies, such as salves, toothpaste, and even skin care products.

 ## Harvesting Beeswax

Beeswax is actually not wax but fatty acids that are highly digestible and extremely good for detoxifying the body when eaten. The bees produce the wax by eating honey, and transform it into beeswax through glands on their abdomens.

Honeycomb can be used or sold as is, with the honey in the beeswax. To harvest beeswax separately, extract the honey from it first, let the bees chew out any leftover honey, and then place the wax cappings in a wax melter. After the wax has been separated out, it can be heated again, like in a crock pot set on low (170 degrees F) and screened through a cloth to filter out any impurities. The beeswax can then be sold or used to make other products such as candles, herbal salves, and lip balms.

Our Home Farms
From Zoe

I am a new top bar beekeeper. I must admit, I traded for bees and inherited them before I was ready for them. I lost two hives as I started out as a beekeeper. I had no previous experience with bees, although I knew them to be an important part of the home farm. The third time I tried to raise bees, I succeeded with a hive that I have now split to create two more hives.

The differences between my successful beekeeping attempts and my unsuccessful ones were educating myself and having a mentor. At first, I had no idea what to look for when I went in to check on the bees, so I just wouldn't open the hive. Months later, I would discover that there was no queen and I had lost the hive. Or I would wait too long to enter the hive until it was such a cross-combed jumble that the work was intimidating and overwhelming. Any time I open up a hive, I find it slightly intimidating, but, like bookkeeping, the longer you put it off, the more intimidating it becomes. Regular hive check-ups (every two weeks or month. depending on the time of year) are essential for successful beekeeping.

Eventually I learned about the lifecycle and the year-cycle of the bees. It is important to know what they are supposed to be doing when. Once you know what is typical, you can more easily notice when something isn't happening as it should.

Finally, I haven't yet found the chunk of time I need to take an in-depth class on beekeeping, so having a mentor has been essential to me. Jessie Brown of Brown's Downtown Bees has taught me what to look for in the hive, how to split a hive, tidy the hive, and replace the queen when necessary.

From Melanie

I started my beekeeping adventure with a nuke hive that Dr. Moses and I had made three weeks earlier. One afternoon in June, we brought hive boxes into my yard and transferred the frames from the nuke box into the hive. It was very exciting, and we actually saw the brand new queen that the honeybees had created in the nuke box.

Throughout the rest of that summer I watered the bees and checked on them periodically. In the beginning I fed them a couple of times with a mixture of half cane sugar and half water. The hive quickly became established and seemed to be humming right along. I had located them in a back corner of my yard, facing east near a cinderblock wall so that they would need to fly up to leave the hive. I also placed them under a pine tree, to the east of my chicken coop, so they would have afternoon shade. They were bordered to the north by another cinderblock wall.

When winter came, this location afforded protection from surrounding winds and falling snow. The winter was a very cold and harsh one, and I wasn't sure they would make it.

When the first warm day of early spring came along, I was thrilled to see them emerging from the hive. They had survived!

In early May, Dr. Moses and I moved the hive to a community garden where I was doing a lot of work. We wanted their presence in that location to pollinate the fruits and vegetables. At the writing of this chapter, the bees are happily and busily working away in the Source Community Garden and surrounding neighborhood, and I am hoping to get a second group of bees to populate a second, top bar hive in the same location.

 Exercise 11.1

Take a few moments to think about whether and how you might want to start a bee hive:

1. Is starting a beehive something you want to do right now?

2. If so, where would you locate it? Would you need to discuss this with your neighbors first, or the people who live in your home with you?

3. Would you start with a Langstroth or top bar hive?

4. Where would you get the necessary equipment? What would it cost you?

5. Where and when would you get your bees?

6. If you don't want to start a hive now, what can you do in your garden to make it more bee-friendly?

Bibliography

Chapter 2:

Kourik, Robert. *Designing and Maintaining Your Edible Landscape Naturally* (Permanent Publications, 2004).

Morrow, Rosemary. *Earth User's Guide to Permaculture; Teacher's Notes* (Kangaroo Press, 2006).

Whitefield, Patrick. *How to Make a Forest Garden* (Permanent Publications, 2002).

Chapter 5:

Kinkade-Levario, Heather. *Design for Water: Rainwater Harvesting, Stormwater Catchment, and Alternate Water Reuse* (New Society Publishers, 2007).

Lancaster, Brad. *Rainwater Harvesting for Drylands* (Rainsource Press, 2006).

Ludwig, Art. *Create an Oasis with Greywater* (Oasis Design, 2006).

Also. *Water Storage: Tanks, Cisterns, Aquifers, and Ponds for Domestic Supply, Fire and Emergency Use--Includes How to Make Ferrocement Water Tanks* (Oasis Design, 2005).

Chapter 7:

Whitefield, Patrick. *How to Make a Forest Garden* (Permanent Publications, 2002).

sunstoneherbs.com for information on plants for an apple guild

Chapter 8:

Hemenway, Toby. *Gaia's Garden; A Guide to Home-Scale Permaculture* (Chelsea Green Publishing, 2001).

Taylor, Lisa. *Your Farm in the City* (Black Dog and Leventhal Publishers, 2011).

Chapter 9:

urbanext.illinois.edu/hortihints for information on collecting and drying tomato seeds.

Chapter 10:

Green-Armytage, Stephen. *Extraordinary Chickens* (Abrams, 2000).

Hobson, J. C. Jeremy. *Keeping Chickens: The Essential Guide to Enjoying and Getting the Best from Chickens* (David & Charles Publishers, 2007).

Kilarski, Barbara. *Keep Chickens! Tending Small Flocks in Cities, Suburbs, and Other Small Spaces* (Story Publishing, 2003).

Lee, Andy W. and Patricia L. Foreman. *Chicken Tractor: The Permaculture Guide to Happy Hens and Healthy Soil* (Good Earth Publications, 1998).

Rossier, Jay. *Living with Chickens: Everything You Need to Know to Raise Your Own Backyard Flock* (Lyons Press, 2004).

http://urbanchickens.org/

http://dukecityfix.com/group/abqurbanchickens

sunstoneherbs.com for herbal chicken remedies.

Chapter 11:

American Apitherapy Society. *Therapy Uses of Bee Products* (AI Root Co., 1997).

Collison, Clarence. *Fundamentals of Beekeeping* (Penn State University, digitized 2008).

Conrad, Ross. *Natural Beekeeping: Organic Approaches to Modern Apiculture* (Chelsea Green Publishing, 2007).

Dadant, CP. *First Lessons in Beekeeping* (Dadant and Sons, 1976).

Delaplane, Keith. *Honeybees and Beekeeping* (University of Georgia, 2006).

Flottum, Kim. *The Backyard Beekeeper* (Quarry Books, 2010).

Grout, Roy A. *The Hive and the Honeybee* (Dadant and Sons, 1992).

Hauk, Gunther. *Toward Saving the Honeybee* (Biodynamic Farming and Gardening Association, 2008).

Hubbell, Sue. *A Book of Bees* (Mariner Books, 1998).

Lauck, Joanne E. *The Voice of the Infinite in the Small* (Swan Raven & Co., 1998).

Other resources:

Suppliers: Mann Lake, Walter T. Kelley, backyardhive.com

Fundraising for Honeybee Preservation, helpthehoneybees.com

Shamanic Work with Bees, sacredtrust.org,

Bee Blog from Albuquerque Beekeeper, mistressbeek.com

Made in the USA
Charleston, SC
17 July 2012